Praise for *Tackling t*

Mike Anderson crafts a compelling case for the claim that motivation for doing the work of learning needs to be owned by the learner. In his usual invitational style, he offers many practical examples that teachers can use to transform the tasks we assign as "school" work into authentically motivated learning opportunities for our students.

—**Bena Kallick**, cofounder and codirector of Institute for Habits of Mind

Have your students ever asked, "Is this going to be graded?" or "Why do we have to do this?" If so, this book is going to save you a lot of headaches and inspire change! In *Tackling the Motivation Crisis,* Mike Anderson explains how many of our current practices, intended to increase engagement, create compliance at best. You will devour this book as you relate to stories about chip theft, beach stone crafts, and how group work and fun are like broccoli. This text, with its practical classroom examples and analogies, will help readers better understand the psychology of motivation, break the cycle of student disinterest, and create equitable opportunities for all students to be self-directed, empowered learners.

—**Katie Novak**, education consultant and best-selling author of *UDL Now, Equity by Design,* and *Innovate Inside the Box*

Mike Anderson's book challenges educators to give up the gimmicks and lean into designing learning experiences with and for students that give them compelling reasons to self-motivate and invest. A must-read for anyone seeking to support the development of authentic, intrinsic motivation in students.

—**Holly Martin**, staff development and professional learning specialist for the Mountain Brook, AL public schools

We've all been there, facing a gauntlet of "unmotivated" and "disengaged" students. We've wished and hoped that something would magically appear to help get them connected and inspired. However, as Mike Anderson points out in *Tackling the Motivation Crisis,* our best bet isn't to try to change the kids, it's to fix a broken system. With a healthy dose of common sense and a plethora of practical ideas, Mike addresses educator mindsets, curriculum, feedback, grading, and discipline—elements of schooling that are under our control—so we might revamp our approaches and tap into our students' innate and intrinsic curiosity. We must do better, and with Mike's guidance, we can.

—**Pete Hall**, former principal and author of *Creating a Culture of Reflective Practice*

As a superintendent of schools, I cannot tell you how many times I've heard from classroom teachers that the students are not motivated to learn. This book is groundbreaking, not because it challenges prevailing behavioral science wisdom, but because it does so while providing teachers an exciting set of practical ideas that can be implemented immediately, something every teacher treasures. Imagine a world where students want to do schoolwork. What a world that would be!

—**Jim Morse**, superintendent of the Oyster River
Cooperative School District, NH

This book is my new go-to guide for deepening student learning! With engaging anecdotes, research findings, and practical strategies, Mike Anderson shows us how to replace the broken system of classroom rewards with a powerful approach that cultivates autonomy, purpose, and joy in our schools.

—**Timothy Walker**, author of *Teach Like Finland:*
33 Simple Strategies for Joyful Classrooms

In *Tackling the Motivation Crisis*, Mike Anderson helps us imagine how to create classrooms in which students truly want to learn, without manipulation or artifice. It is a guide we all need to help us help students change from compliant to self-motivated learners.

—**Carl Anderson**, author and literacy consultant

TACKLING THE MOTIVATION CRISIS

Also by Mike Anderson

What We Say and How We Say It Matter: Teacher Talk That Improves Student Learning and Behavior

Learning to Choose, Choosing to Learn: The Key to Student Motivation and Achievement

The Well-Balanced Teacher: How to Work Smarter and Stay Sane Inside the Classroom and Out

Teacher Talk That Matters (Quick Reference Guide)

TACKLING THE MOTIVATION CRISIS

How to Activate Student Learning
Without Behavior Charts, Pizza Parties,
or Other Hard-to-Quit Incentive Systems

MIKE ANDERSON

ascd

Alexandria, Virginia USA

1703 N. Beauregard St. • Alexandria, VA 22311-1714 USA
Phone: 800-933-2723 or 703-578-9600 • Fax: 703-575-5400
Website: www.ascd.org • Email: member@ascd.org
Author guidelines: www.ascd.org/write

Ranjit Sidhu, *CEO & Executive Director;* Penny Reinart, *Chief Impact Officer;* Genny Ostertag, *Senior Director, Acquisitions & Editing;* Julie Houtz, *Director, Book Editing;* Liz Wegner, *Editor;* Thomas Lytle, *Creative Director;* Donald Ely, *Art Director;* Georgia Park, *Senior Graphic Designer;* Keith Demmons, *Senior Production Designer;* Kelly Marshall, *Production Manager;* Shajuan Martin, *E-Publishing Specialist*

All web links in this book are correct as of the publication date below but may have become inactive or otherwise modified since that time. If you notice a deactivated or changed link, please email books@ascd.org with the words "Link Update" in the subject line. In your message, please specify the web link, the book title, and the page number on which the link appears.

PAPERBACK ISBN: 978-1-4166-3033-3   ASCD product #121033 n8/21
PDF E-BOOK ISBN: 978-1-4166-3034-0; see Books in Print for other formats.
Quantity discounts are available: email programteam@ascd.org or call 800-933-2723, ext. 5773, or 703-575-5773. For desk copies, go to www.ascd.org/deskcopy.

Library of Congress Cataloging-in-Publication Data
Names: Anderson, Mike, 1971- author.
Title: Tackling the motivation crisis : how to activate student learning
   without behavior charts, pizza parties, or other hard-to-quit incentive
   systems / Mike Anderson.
Description: Alexandria, VA : ASCD, 2021. | Includes bibliographical
   references and index.
Identifiers: LCCN 2021016575 (print) | LCCN 2021016576 (ebook) | ISBN
   9781416630333 (paperback) | ISBN 9781416630340 (pdf)
Subjects: LCSH: Motivation in education. | Classroom management.
Classification: LCC LB1065 .A6333 2021 (print) | LCC LB1065 (ebook) | DDC
   371.95/6--dc23
LC record available at https://lccn.loc.gov/2021016575
LC ebook record available at https://lccn.loc.gov/2021016576

30 29 28 27 26 25 24 23 22   2 3 4 5 6 7 8 9 10 11 12

TACKLING THE MOTIVATION CRISIS

1

A Motivation Crisis

We have a motivation crisis in our schools.

Across the United States, far too many kids don't want to do schoolwork. You see it in their tired and listless expressions in class. You hear it from parents who struggle to get them to do homework. Teachers often lament, "These kids just don't want to do anything! They're so unmotivated!" In fact, as I work in schools across the United States, this is the most often-voiced frustration I hear from teachers, especially in upper grades: "Kids today just don't care about school." According to a 2014 Gallup poll of more than 800,000 students, nearly half (47 percent) reported being either not engaged or actively disengaged in school (Collier, 2015). Another survey conducted that same year, this one by *Education Week,* asked teachers and administrators about student motivation, and only 40 percent of those surveyed believed their students were "highly engaged and motivated" (Collier, 2015). These are just a couple of such surveys that seem to reveal how far too many children don't seem motivated or invested in their schoolwork.

Chances are, you have your own experiences that confirm this. Perhaps at home, your own children seem bored or detached from learning in school. You might have had this experience when you were a kid. I certainly did. And when you look at the students in your classroom, though some of them are motivated and excited to learn, you can probably immediately picture the ones who aren't. They sit with blank stares, peeking at their phones whenever your back is turned. They don't turn in work, and when they do, it seems as if they've done the least amount possible. Or they disrupt by agitating other kids in class who are ready and eager to learn. They're the ones that keep you up at night.

There are obvious and clear correlations between motivation and achievement. In a different Gallup poll, this one conducted in 2016, students who were actively disengaged are nine times more likely to say they get bad grades, twice as likely to say they miss days of school, and more than seven times more likely to say they feel discouraged about the future as compared with students who say they are engaged. What's especially troubling is that motivation for learning seems to drop as students get older. Although 74 percent of 5th graders report being engaged, 18 percent as not engaged, and only 8 percent as actively disengaged, by the time students are well into high school, about one-third of students say they are engaged while two-thirds are either not engaged or actively disengaged (Calderon & Yu, 2017).

Although this certainly isn't a new phenomenon, the COVID-19 pandemic seemed to make things worse. As schools across the globe shut down and learning moved online, even more students seemed to struggle with engagement. According to a survey of 1,150 district leaders, principals, and teachers conducted by the EdWeek Research Center, by the end of 2019–2020 school year, teachers' top challenge was students not even logging in for school or interacting with them at all. A whopping 66 percent of respondents cited this as a major challenge (Kurtz, 2020). In a different survey, this one taken by 20,438 students in 166 public schools across nine states during May and June of 2020, we again see how differences in motivation played out when learning moved home during the COVID-19 crisis. Fifty-seven percent of 5th graders said they could motivate themselves to do schoolwork while just over one-quarter of high school seniors could do so (YouthTruth Student Survey, 2020).

So there's no doubt we have a motivation crisis, but I'm actually not convinced it's as bleak as (or as seemingly impossible to tackle as) the data I've just cited suggest. Although there's no doubt that these surveys and studies reveal a disheartening lack of motivation for and engagement with schoolwork, does this mean that our students are truly unmotivated? Or is it more accurate to say that they're unmotivated to do the work we're giving them (and the way in which we're framing it)? It's very possible that we have highly motivated students who display low motivation for schoolwork. Resisting schoolwork that doesn't feel relevant, interesting, or fun might actually be a sign that students haven't become overly compliant.

My son is a perfect example. I remember one afternoon when he was in high school, he was not doing his assigned physics homework. Instead, he was building an air cannon (made from PVC pipe, a bicycle pump, and an irrigation valve) that could fire a foam dart over the roof of our house. He spent hours perfecting the cannon until the dart fired so high you couldn't see it anymore. So while he was blowing off his physics homework, he was engaging in a hands-on physics project. He was highly motivated—just not to do the work his teacher assigned.

The fact that motivation for schoolwork seems to drop as students get older is especially a problem because motivation is one of the most highly valued attributes of employees in our new economy. If you want to conduct an interesting experiment, try an internet search for "skills wanted in the workplace" (or some variation of that). Check out the first few resources that come up and scan for words such as *initiative, motivational skills, strong work values, strong work ethic, self-management,* and *commitment.* Businesses, for the most part, are not looking for people who want to punch in, punch out, and do the least amount required of them. They're looking for people who are self-motivated. They also don't want someone who needs constant hand-holding and managing—they want people who can manage themselves. I was speaking at an event for parents at a wealthy private school in Los Angeles. The talk was about social-emotional learning (SEL) skills needed for effective learning and was part of the school's effort to help parents understand the need for the teaching of SEL skills as a part of daily academics. I asked for a show of hands: "How many of you help with the hiring process—at least in some form—at the businesses where you work?" Nearly all of the hands went up. "And are you looking to hire people who need to be managed and motivated, or are you looking for people who are self-motivated and self-managing?" The consensus was clear. No one wants to hire someone who will need constant supervision or external motivation.

And yet, what does it typically take to be good at school? Usually, it means that students are really good at doing what they're told. They complete assignments and turn them in on time—to the specifications of the teacher. They learn the content that is required as determined by the curriculum. They follow the rules set by the teacher or school. In short, they're compliant. Although they are successful, according to the ways we often measure success in schools, these are also students we should worry about. They seem motivated, but they're not really self-motivated. They are eager to get the grades they (or their parents) want, but they don't seem interested in the learning itself. "Is this graded?" is their way of saying, "Should I care about this?" If the answer is yes, they want to know exactly what they have to do to get the grade they want—which can be really hard when an assignment involves creativity, complex reasoning, or other high-level thinking. So we send them confusing messages like "Of course the grade is important, but don't care about it too much. I also want you to be curious and excited about the learning!" After all, we don't really want kids who are grade-grubbers, do we? Don't we want students who are driven from within when it comes to their work and learning? Remember the YouthTruth survey, which showed how kids struggled with motivation when learning went remote during spring of 2020? In the summary of the survey results, there are representative comments that reflect students' most common sentiments based on the number and type of keywords. They had one representative comment under the heading *Motivation:*

> Finding the motivation to do schoolwork was the most difficult challenge I found during distance learning. In a classroom, most of the time, you are forced to work on assignments either as a class or in a small group of friends. At home, you have to push yourself to be productive. Lacking motivation caused me to dramatically fall behind.

These compliant kids—students who are good at playing the school game but aren't really developing interests or gaining skills in self-management and self-motivation—should also worry us. Being compliant is no longer a highly sought-after attribute in the world of work.

They don't often rise to the top of our worry-about list, though, because the ones who aren't compliant occupy so much of our time and energy. These students have a tough row to hoe. They become labeled as problems or troublemakers, and their journeys through school are rough. In a stunning and incisive rebuke of the status quo in schools, educator and author Carla Shalaby forces us to challenge this norm in schools: "In school we generally identify the most pleasant, most compliant children as our leaders. But if being a leader means doing exactly as one is told, we should wonder what it means to be a follower" (2017, p. xviii). Instead, she encourages us to view troublemakers as "canaries in coal mines," children who warn us of conditions that might be unhealthy. They are placed in punitive time-outs or get removed from classrooms for moving too much or talking too much. They lose valuable learning time and are sent a clear message: "You don't belong here." Not surprisingly, they often then struggle more academically. There are also children who come to school and struggle academically, and as they too pick up messages that they aren't good enough and that they don't belong (as they're separated from peers to receive "special" instruction and given failing grades for poor work), many of them begin to act out. Feeling frustrated and stupid and isolated, they fight back, becoming disruptive and exerting energy to avoid work at all costs. This is the circular nature of behavior and academic challenges. One begets the other. Perhaps we shouldn't be surprised that as students experience more school, many of them become less and less engaged.

It seems like it shouldn't be this way, though, doesn't it? Can't we imagine it happening a different way? Can't we imagine kids getting *more* fired up and passionate about learning the more school they experience? That being in buildings and online learning spaces dedicated to learning, surrounded by adults who are excited to facilitate learning, they would get more turned on to learning, not less? Can't we imagine that, as content gets more complex, it could get more interesting, not less? That as kids get older, they develop more skills of self-management and self-motivation?

This may feel especially perplexing as we consider how much time, how much energy, and how many resources we use trying to motivate students' academic work and behavior. Grades are just one example of the myriad of motivational tools and strategies we use in schools: Sticker and star reward systems, student of the week/month programs, pizza for reading in the summer, good citizenship awards, marbles, and gems in jars are but a few more. These token economy systems—if you do x, then you get y (a sticker, grade, point, etc.)—are so widely used that it's hard to find schools where they aren't used in some capacity in all parts of the United States, in wealthy districts and poor ones; in rural, urban, and suburban ones; in private, independent, and public schools; in preschools and high schools.

With all of these systems designed to motivate students and manage their behavior, shouldn't we see kids getting more engaged and excited about school, not less, as they get older? If these systems work as we think they do, shouldn't motivation be going up and behavior be getting better as kids experience more of them?

What if these systems are having the reverse of their intended effect? What if they're making students less motivated instead of more? I used one of these token economy systems early in my career, and I got to experience firsthand both why they are so alluring and how they can backfire.

My Experience with Incentive Systems: Chips for Pizza

I was so proud of my classroom management system at the beginning of my first year of teaching. Students in my class sat in pods of four desks pulled together. Each of these groups was like a mini-team, and each pod had a small plastic butter tub (cleaned, of course). I walked around with a pocketful of small purple cardboard disks that we called chips. When students were doing what they should—cooperating, working hard, sharing materials, and so on—I might pass by and toss a couple of chips into their container. Individual students could also gain chips for their team by focusing well, working hard, asking a good question, or doing a kind deed. Students could lose them, too. If a group was quarreling or getting off task, I might come by and remove a chip or two. If a student said something mean or forgot to bring in their homework, they might also lose a chip for their group. The goal for the groups was to get to 75 chips. If they could accomplish this, I would take the group out for a pizza lunch at the family-owned Italian restaurant right next to the school.

Can you imagine how excited my students were when I first introduced this system? They cheered and clapped at the idea of going out for pizza for lunch. The system worked brilliantly—at first. As I walked around the classroom, kids would straighten up in their chairs, sometimes even folding their hands and batting their eyelashes playfully. When I tossed chips into the dishes, kids beamed, often smiling at each other and basking in their success. If a group was getting off task, all I had to do was catch someone's eye and pat my pocket or start to move in their direction, and they'd get back on track. When groups started accumulating enough chips for a pizza lunch, we had a blast. Eating lunch together and sitting in a booth at a family restaurant felt so exciting, and it was such a wonderful way to build relationships with them and between them.

After a while, though, some elements of the systems started to trouble me. Some students started to get sneaky. I'd be walking around the room, and I'd hear someone warn their tablemates in a frantic whisper, "Shhh! He's coming!" Table groups started accusing each other of chip theft: "Hey! We counted our chips before recess, and we had 57. Now we only have 38! I think Laura's table took some of ours!" Kids also started to gang up on individuals at their tables—kids who already struggled. "Billy?! You didn't do your homework again?! Great! Now we're never going to get pizza!" To be honest, this was part of the idea of the system. I had wanted kids to hold each other accountable, but when I heard this negative peer pressure actually happening, I didn't like the feeling of it. Neither did Billy. I started to get the sense that he (and a few others) sometimes intentionally sabotaged a group by misbehaving on purpose—just to get them mad.

There were other problems. I was good at remembering the chips early in the year, but as the year got going, I sometimes forgot. Kids reminded me, "Mr. A.? Don't we get some chips? We were working really well." Some tables who struggled to get enough chips for pizza just gave up. They decided the effort wasn't worth the work, and then their motivation and behavior seemed to get worse. After all, if the goal was to get pizza, and they had decided the pizza didn't matter enough, why bother trying?

Perhaps the most troubling aspect of the system was that it didn't mesh with my beliefs about teaching and learning or the positive goals I had for my students. I wanted my students to be kind and respectful because that was how we would form a safe and vibrant learning community, not because they wanted pizza. I wanted them to work hard and engage in learning because they were curious and self-motivated, not because they were being motivated by me. I believed that school and learning should be inherently interesting, but what did it mean if I thought my students needed to look forward to pizza to be interested in school?

These systems of extrinsic motivation and management are so ubiquitous that they go unquestioned and unchallenged in many places, but as you'll see in the next chapter, my experience isn't unique. These systems often have short-term payoffs with long-term consequences.

Boost Student Motivation: Three Action Steps

So here we are, stuck in a vicious cycle of kids experiencing systems and strategies of motivation that make things worse. This makes them appear less motivated, so we double down and try even harder to motivate them—which, again, just makes it worse. It's time to break the cycle. It's time to stop trying to motivate our students and instead create school experiences that allow students to be self-motivated. That's what this book is all about. In the pages that follow, you will learn the three key steps we need to take to make this happen.

Step 1: Stop Incentivizing Students

As you'll see in Chapters 2 and 3, the more time and energy we spend trying to motivate our students' learning and behavior through extrinsic means—pizza parties, gem jars, behavior charts, traditional grading systems, teacher-pleasing praise, and other such incentive systems—the less intrinsic motivation they will have. We need to stop using these systems.

Step 2: Tap into Students' Intrinsic Motivators

The second step is deceptively simple. We need to make sure students' academic work is compelling and interesting enough that they will want to do it. Chapter 4 illustrates how we can activate student learning through six intrinsic motivators. These are motivators that all students walk into school with, and we can embed them in any lesson, activity, project, or unit.

Step 3: Teach Students Skills of Self-Management

Although getting rid of incentive systems and tapping into students' intrinsic motivators will help students become more self-motivated, those two things aren't enough. Even the most self-motivated learners have struggles. Even the most interesting project gets boring at times. Students need to know how to push through challenges, manage frustration, and overcome being overwhelmed. In Chapter 5, you will explore a wide array of strategies to teach to students so they can become more skilled at self-management, which will help them follow through on their self-motivation.

Chapters 6, 7, and 8 will help you see how this looks in action in three practical realms of school: curricula and instruction (Chapter 6), feedback and assessment (Chapter 7), and discipline and classroom management (Chapter 8). You'll gain a wide variety of practical examples, concrete strategies, and ideas to use that will help you integrate many of the ideas presented in Chapters 2–5.

There is no one "right" way to shift from systems of extrinsic motivation to ones of intrinsic motivation, so in Chapter 9, you'll learn several important ideas and strategies to try. You'll hear how many educators have managed to make these shifts, including how I ditched the "chips for pizza" system.

So let's get started. We need to begin by understanding how incentive systems might help us manage students in the short term while doing immense damage to students' motivation and learning in the long term. We need to understand what's wrong with incentives.

2

What's Wrong with Incentives

We use incentive and reward systems—even ones that perhaps feel punitive—with the best of intentions. We're trying to support students' learning and positive behavior. We're hoping to motivate and inspire students to work hard and do well in school. We may even see these systems as a way of building relationships with our students and helping them feel good about themselves. Most of us have probably used or tried them at some point or another. They seem to make so much sense. How could they possibly be a bad thing for kids?

What's tricky about motivation is that it's not as straightforward as we might think. We probably think of motivation in a linear, almost mathematical, way. If you already have some motivation, and you are given more incentives, than you'll end up even more motivated. Two plus two equals four. As it turns out, in the world of motivation, the use of extrinsic motivators can lead to counterintuitive results. Sometimes, two plus two equals one (or even negative five).

Have You Seen Any of These Things Happen?

There's a good chance that you have seen some of the nonlinear and counterintuitive effects of incentive systems in action. Do any of these examples sound familiar?

- Students who get pizza gift certificates for reading books decide to read the shortest and easiest books possible to get more pizza.
- A class that was energized and excited about earning stars toward a movie in September no longer seems to care so much in January.
- Students cheat on tests and quizzes to get grades that don't reflect their learning.
- Even though your goal is for students to be responsible for the sake of each other, they ask, "What will I get for it?" when you ask them to help clean the room.
- Students ask, "Is this graded?" before they decide if an assignment is worth the effort.
- You have to keep offering more and more "class bucks" to get kids to clean up the room and be kind to each other as the year goes on.

What's going on here? Why don't rewards and other incentives work the way we think they will? What is it about these systems and strategies that lead to such varying and confusing behaviors?

Incentives Undermine Intrinsic Motivation

As we consider the main purpose of this book—to help boost students' self-motivation—perhaps the most damning side effect of incentives is that they tend to undermine intrinsic motivation. Researchers Deci, Koestner, and Ryan (1999) pored through 128 studies that explored the effects of extrinsic rewards on motivation. They found that rewards significantly undermined intrinsic motivation. They found especially overwhelming evidence that contingent rewards (if you do x, then you'll get y) did big-time damage to both intrinsic motivation and interest. In a synthesis of four meta-analyses, researchers explored the impact that grades had on both academic motivation and achievement, as opposed to comments or no performance feedback at all. Not only did grades have a negative impact on achievement and motivation as compared to comments, grades were shown to have a negative effect on motivation as compared with no feedback whatsoever. That's right. *Students who received no feedback at all had more motivation than ones given grades* (Koenka et al., 2019).

Even though the primary reason we use incentives—either the promise of rewards or the threat of punishments—is to increase students' motivation, they often have the reverse effect. This happens for a few reasons: satiation, crowding out, and signaling.

Satiation

If you've ever used incentives and rewards in school, you've likely seen this play out. When you introduced the idea of earning an ice cream party or getting school bucks to spend at the school store, students probably cheered. For a few days or weeks, this enthusiasm might have kept students going. Then motivation faded as the luster of the prizes wore off. This is one of the most common side effects of extrinsic motivators, and it's called *satiation*. Once kids have earned a few stickers (or pizza slices, pencils, etc.), the allure fades.

Now you're left with two unappealing options. One is to drop the incentive altogether. If you do, be prepared for a significant drop in motivation at first. Study after study after study has found that when extrinsic incentives are used and then removed, intrinsic motivation drops:

- Four-year-olds who liked to draw were given incentives to draw during free choice time. After the incentives were removed, they drew dramatically less on their own for pleasure (Lepper, Greene, & Nisbett, 1973).
- When people are incentivized with matching funds to donate to public goods, donations go up in the short term but then drop back down below where they were before the incentive was offered in the long run (Meier, 2007).
- Financial rewards do seem to help people quit smoking in the short term, but "no research has shown that financial rewards produce improvement in the number of people who succeed in quitting smoking entirely" (Redmond & Solomon, 2007, p. 3).

So if you drop the incentives, be ready to be patient as students recalibrate.

The other option is to up the ante. If stickers are no longer appealing, maybe candy will work. Once candy doesn't cut it, maybe you can offer toys or cash. One teacher shared a story with me about how he used "schollars" (a mash-up of *scholar* and *dollars*) to motivate his students, but he kept having to offer more and more as the year went on. Another teacher (one who worked in a wealthy private school) told me a story about the out-of-control inflation of incentives with one of her students. As the allure of nicer and nicer offers failed to motivate his son, a dad offered his 4th grader Lakers tickets if he would do his homework one night. This is what it looks like when the ante keeps getting upped, and it highlights why satiation is such a problem when it comes to incentives and motivation.

Crowding Out

A few years ago, I began making beach stone crafts as a hobby. I'd head to the beach to look for smooth stones with vibrant colors to create wall hooks, necklaces, cabinet knobs, business card holders, and my favorite, wine stoppers. Learning these new crafts gave me a sense of mastery and accomplishment, and after I had been at it awhile, trying some craft fairs seemed like the next logical step. After all, the cost for supplies for the crafts was adding up, I had a lot of crafts I didn't know what to do with, and craft fairs offered me a new sense of purpose. In three fairs one holiday season I made more than $1,000—enough to buy a nice tile saw and plenty more materials. I was thrilled! Then came the Etsy shop, which, again, seemed like a logical next step. If I was going to keep making some money, I needed to sell crafts online. Several orders came in right away.

It was all so exciting—until it wasn't.

The change happened gradually. As I was drilling a hole in a stone for a pendant, instead of marveling at the flecks of color as they emerged from the stone, I'd find myself wondering how much time I was spending and what my hourly rate would be. Trips to the beach became more targeted ("I'm going to try to find 20 new wine stopper stones"), which made them less enjoyable. I had to claim the income from my hobby on my tax return. My energy for the hobby faded as it felt less like play and more like a chore. It's been quite awhile now since I have done any stonework.

This is what it feels like when one motivation crowds out another. My initial motivation came from the joy of going to the beach, working with the stones themselves, and the sense of accomplishment and purpose I found in making crafts for friends and family. Then my purpose shifted. At first, the addition of money to the equation boosted my enthusiasm. It was exciting to create business cards and start an Etsy shop, but I allowed the business side of the work to overtake the pleasure of the work itself. I started getting my sense of satisfaction and purpose from making money. Then, when I created a craft that didn't sell, I felt defeated. Even when I did sell items, the excitement faded over time. Selling a wine stopper for $20 didn't feel like such a big deal after I'd sold a bunch of them.

In the field of psychology, this is called *crowding out.* When there's already intrinsic motivation (love of reading, interest in science, drive to get better as a musician, sense of autonomy and purpose in a research project) and an extrinsic motivator is added (monetary incentive, stickers, pizza party, grades), intrinsic motivation fades.

Signaling

Incentives also send confusing messages about what we value. The person offered the incentive may wonder, "If this was worth doing on its own, why would I need to be motivated to do it?" In one study involving middle schoolers who were given awards for attendance, the month after they were given awards, students' absenteeism increased by 8 percent. The awards sent an unintended signal: School must not be worth going to on its own if I need to be rewarded for going (Robinson, Gallus, Lee, & Rogers, 2019).

One researcher explains signaling this way:

> People are often unsure about what the best course of action is and consequently seek clues from the environment.... For example, if you are unsure whether solving puzzles is fun and someone offers you $5 per puzzle solved, you might reasonably infer that this activity is not enjoyable and thus forgo it, even though you might have tried and enjoyed solving the puzzles in the absence of a monetary incentive. (Kamenica, 2012, p. 429)

This is called *signaling*. Without meaning to, when we use incentives, we may signal to students that good behavior or good work aren't worth doing on their own.

To see this phenomenon in action, I highly recommend checking out a clip from a 1996 episode of the *Oprah Winfrey Show* (www.youtube.com/watch?v=_6wwReKUYmw). In a replication of other studies, 20 teenagers are each brought in to solve puzzles for a fictitious toy company. Half are paid to solve puzzles, and the other half aren't. Nine of 10 kids who were paid to solve puzzles, stopped playing with the puzzles as soon as they were paid. *All 10* of the kids who weren't paid continued to play with the puzzles even after they were told their job was finished because they found the puzzles interesting or fun or challenging (Valiante, 2013). It's a fascinating illustration of how extrinsic motivators can undermine intrinsic motivation.

Incentives Diminish Learning and Performance

So incentives can backfire when it comes to motivation, but what does this mean about actual learning and performance? After all, if incentives reduce intrinsic motivation, but students learn more anyway, perhaps the trade-off is worth it.

In fact, there is a sizeable body of evidence that suggests that incentives actually diminish learning and performance, just like they reduce intrinsic motivation.

Edward Deci, one of the cocreators of *self-determination theory* (SDT), wanted to better understand the connection between grades—one of the most widely used extrinsic motivators in schools—and motivation and learning. He and his research team designed a study where two groups of college students worked at learning complex science content. One group was told they would take a test and be graded on their learning, and the other group was told they would teach others what they had learned. As they expected, when they gave everyone a survey at the end, the group working for grades reported less intrinsic motivation for the task. Then they gave all students from both groups a test—a test that half of them had been studying for.

The results showed that the students who learned in order to put the material to active use displayed considerably greater conceptual understanding of the material than did the students who learned in order to be tested. As the research made clear, yet again, well-intentioned people—for instance, people employing tests to motivate learning—are unwittingly defeating the desire to learn in those people they are attempting to help. (Deci, 1995, pp. 47–48)

In a summary of research, Deci and colleague Richard Ryan (the other cocreator of SDT) conclude that "comparisons between people whose motivation is authentic (literally self-authored or endorsed) and those who are merely externally controlled for an action typically reveal that the former, relative to the latter, have more interest, excitement, and confidence, which in turn is manifest both as enhanced performance, persistence, and creativity" (Ryan & Deci, 2000, p. 69).

John Hattie's book *Visible Learning* is a meta-analysis of *more than 800 meta-analyses* relating to achievement. In his discussion of feedback in the classroom, he offers the following indictment of extrinsic motivators: "Programmed instruction, praise, punishment, and extrinsic rewards were the least effective forms of feedback for enhancing achievement. Indeed, it is doubtful whether rewards should be thought of as feedback at all" (Hattie, 2009, p. 174).

Alfie Kohn's groundbreaking book *Punished by Rewards,* first published in 1993, offers a thorough and conclusive examination of numerous studies about extrinsic motivation and shows how they both undermine intrinsic motivation and diminish productivity. On the 25th anniversary of this revolutionary book, he concluded, "I reviewed as many studies as I could find that were conducted since its original publication. The conclusions that rewards frequently kill both interest and excellence have, if anything, grown more solid in the intervening decades" (Kohn, 2018, para. 5).

Although the research on the connection between online learning and motivation isn't yet as robust as we might wish, some similarities to more traditional in-school learning are emerging. In studies involving Massive Open Online Courses (MOOCs), motivation has been linked to both student engagement and performance (de Barba, Kennedy, & Ainley, 2016; Sujatha & Kavitha, 2018). One study has also found that students with intrinsic motivational dispositions performed better in MOOCs than did students who were extrinsically motivated (Moore & Wang, 2021).

Choking

One of the most commonly held beliefs about rewards and incentives seems to be that higher incentives will lead to greater results. By this point, you can probably predict the reality, though, that the reverse is true. The pressure of high rewards or the worry about severe punishments can lead to worse performance—a phenomenon commonly known as choking under pressure (Yu, 2015). Sian Beilock has written an entire book about the subject, *Choke: What the Secrets of the Brain Reveal About Getting It Right When You Have To*, and study after study she conducted and that she cites shows the potential detrimental effects of high pressure on performance (2010).

So when, in our well-meaning attempt to help kids care more, we incentivize—either through the promise of greater rewards or the threat of harsher punishments—we make it harder for many children to be successful. Many studies have even shown direct correlations between the size of a reward offered and performance—and in the exact opposite ways most people would anticipate: Higher rewards lead to lower performance (Pink, 2009, pp. 40–42).

Lowered Creativity

Have you seen the TV show *Whose Line Is It Anyway?* An improv comedy game show, it involves four contestants (comedians who appear regularly on the show) who are given tasks involving quick thinking and creativity. For example, they might have to sing an impromptu song in a certain style (e.g., country) pulled from a hat about a topic (e.g., toothbrushes) suggested from an audience member. Or they might all need to act out a scene without any prep time based on audience suggestions or the whim of the host.

My favorite game they play is called Props. Contestants are given random props, and in partnerships, they have to come up with as many ridiculous uses for the props as quickly as they can. Giant pink inflatable lollipops become in quick succession snail antennae, a hobby horse (ridden by the president), a Tron motorcycle, oars for a canoe, tennis rackets, and a game spinner that points a contestant to an audience member for a kiss. A six-foot tall purple rubber plunger becomes the Olympic torch, a sword, a trout with its tongue out, the crow's nest of a ship, and a bell in a clock tower.

The creativity of the comedians is breathtaking. They come up with ideas that are goofy and incongruous, and it's the unexpected that makes the game so good. This incongruity—finding novel and surprising ways to use props—makes us laugh. Creativity isn't just for the world of improv comedy shows, though. It's one of the most sought-after skills in the workplace.

George Land was a general systems scientist who spent his career studying creative performance. In a 2011 TEDX talk, he explained a study he conducted at the request of NASA, which was looking for a way to select their most creative people. The test that Land and his team created was simple, so he decided to give it to 1,600 4- and 5-year-old children to see what would happen. He and his research team were shocked to find that 98 percent of the children scored in the genius range of the test. Five years later, they tested the same children, but this time only 30 percent of them scored in the genius range. Five years later, most of these now 15-year-olds were even less creative: only 12 percent of them scored at the highest level. Since then, this test has been given to thousands of adults, and on average, only about 2 percent of adults score at the range that most kindergartners did (Land, 2011). The late (and great) educator, author, and speaker Ken Robinson offered an explanation of this phenomenon: "A lot of things have happened to these kids as they've grown up. A lot. But one of the most important things that has happened to them, I'm convinced, is that by now they have become educated. They've spent 10 years being told there's one answer—it's at the back. And don't look" (RSA, 2010).

I think that is part of what's happened, but I think there's something beyond fixating on not making mistakes that has also dampened children's creativity. These kids have also spent years being incentivized, and as it turns out, incentivization kills creativity. Dan Pink highlights this point in *Drive*, as he explains why rewards increase the amount of time it took people to solve a puzzle involving attaching a candle to a wall—a puzzle that requires creative thinking to solve. "Rewards, by their very nature, narrow our focus. That's helpful when there is a clear path to a solution. They help us stare ahead and race faster. But 'if-then' motivators are terrible for challenges like the candle problem" (2009, p. 44).

You might be wondering, *What about* Whose Line Is It Anyway? *It's a TV game show. There must be points and prizes. Wouldn't that seem to contradict this notion that incentives diminish creativity?* Funny you should ask. As the host, Aisha Tyler, introduces the show, she says, "Welcome to *Whose Line Is It Anyway?* where everything is made up and the points don't matter!" Throughout the game, she liberally and arbitrarily gives away (and subtracts) points, as the contestants shrug and chuckle. (They never actually keep score.) A "winner" is announced at the end of each show, but this is also random, and there is no cash or any other kind of prize. If producers were to change the show to include real points and prizes, they would almost certainly diminish the creativity of the contestants and make the show dramatically less funny.

There's an important side note that should be mentioned here, for it's a question that often emerges. These comedians participating on *Whose Line Is It Anyway?* are getting paid to be on the show. Isn't that a kind of incentive? They wouldn't do the work for free, would they?

Dan Pink also answers this very question. He explains that when organizations structure pay so that it's directly tied to performance (e.g., bonuses and incentives for productivity or creativity), that's when money demotivates. However, "effective organizations compensate people in ways that allow individuals to mostly forget about compensation and instead focus on the work itself" (2009, p. 170). So if players' performances were directly tied to the on-the-spot creativity, they would probably be *less creative* because they'd be worried about the money.

Incentives Suppress the Use of Other Strategies

When behaviorists encourage the use of a token economy system for a student or a group of students, the ultimate goal is (or should be) to eventually remove the stars, stickers, or tokens so that the child can learn to function independently. In my experience in schools, this almost never happens, especially with broad-based classroomwide or schoolwide token economy systems. Instead of the incentive plan being a part of a broader system, these plans often *become* the system. When I ask teachers what the plan is for moving away from these systems, I usually find that there isn't one. The plan isn't to use the incentive to establish better behavior patterns and then move away from them—the plan is to use the behavior systems to continually manage students' behaviors. Because there isn't an exit strategy, the actual teaching of self-management skills (which we will dig into in Chapter 5) gets shortchanged.

Behavior charts, gem jars, my "chips for pizza" plan, and other token economy systems oversimplify teaching. Instead of emphasizing building relationships and teaching self-management skills, the tokens become the focus. Grading can have the same impact when the grades are given as the primary motivation for learning. We may tell a student to study for a test while shortchanging the teaching of the skills needed to study effectively or take a test well. Revolutionary educator Bill Ayers warns against this oversimplification of teaching in his memoir, *To Teach*:

> Teaching as the direct delivery of some preplanned curriculum, teaching as the orderly and scripted conveyance of information, teaching as clerking, is simply a myth. Teaching is much larger and more alive than that; it contains more pain and conflict, more joy and intelligence, more uncertainty and ambiguity. It requires more judgement and energy and intensity than, on some days, seems humanly possible. Teaching is spectacularly unlimited. (1993, p. 5)

Incentives Lower Moral Reasoning and Academic Engagement

Developmental psychologist Lawrence Kohlberg devoted much of his professional life to understanding the development of moral thinking in children. The framework in Figure 2.1 is based on his work (1981) as well an adaptation of his work that I offer in *What We Say and How We Say It Matter*

(Anderson, 2019). It shows various levels of moral reasoning, from ones that are fairly low (avoiding punishment and gaining rewards or praise) to higher-level ones such as following agreed-upon rules and respecting others. I recommend reading this chart from the bottom up.

FIGURE 2.1

Hierarchy of Moral Reasoning

Level of Moral Reasoning	Description	Driving Question
Respecting all people	At this highest stage, people are concerned with taking care of others and the greater good.	"How will my actions impact others?"
Following rules	In this higher stage, people are concerned with order and the functioning of the group.	"What if everybody did it?"
Earning praise/recognition	Here, people are motivated by social recognition and relationships.	"What will people think of me?"
Gaining a reward	This level is still quite self-centered. Here, people consider possible rewards as the goal.	"What's in it for me?"
Avoiding punishment	In the lowest level of moral reasoning, people consider avoiding punishment as the primary goal.	"Will I get in trouble?"

In my experience as an educator, it's quite clear that the vast majority of us want kids to develop higher-level moral reasoning. We want students to be kind, considerate, polite, compassionate, honest, and trustworthy, and to do so because they are thinking of others, not because they're worried about punishments or rewards.

What if we were to create a similar hierarchy for academic engagement? At the lowest levels, students might be actively disengaged or apathetic.

At the higher levels, students would be more actively engaged and self-motivated. Again, consider examining Figure 2.2 from the bottom up.

FIGURE 2.2		
Hierarchy of Academic Engagement		
Level of Academic Engagement	**Description**	**How Students Feel**
Self-Motivation	At this highest stage, students do something even if it's not on the learning agenda. They have a hard time stopping to move on to other tasks.	"I find this inherently interesting and enjoyable. I'm fired up, and you can't stop me!"
Engagement	In this higher level, students have more enthusiasm and energy for their work.	"This matters to me, and it fits with what I care about."
Compliance	Here, students do what they're supposed to do, because they're supposed to.	"I'll do what you say."
Apathy	Barely better than refusal, students' goal here is to do the least amount possible.	"I'll do the bare minimum because you're making me."
Refusal	In the lowest level of engagement, students flat out refuse to do work.	"I won't do it, and you can't make me."

So how does the use of extrinsic motivators potentially affect students' moral reasoning and academic engagement? Once again, we return to the idea of signaling. What signals are we sending to students when we use incentives to try and motivate academic engagement and positive behavior? They are probably not the messages we intend.

Transactional Learning and Behavior

One evening, I was hanging out in the kitchen with my son, Ethan, who at the time was a junior in high school. "You have a physics test tomorrow, don't you?" I asked. "Yeah," he responded, sounding a trifle proud, "I actually studied for this one." "Really? For how long?" I asked. "Like, a half-hour," he responded. Something about my body language or facial expression must have revealed that I thought this wasn't enough. He held up his hand to stop me from saying anything. "Look, Dad. I've already studied enough to get a *B*. To get an *A*, I'd have to study like another 8 to 10 hours, and I'm sorry, but 10 points is not worth 8 to 10 hours." Now, it's debatable as to whether an extra 10 points really would have required that much time, but I got his point. Learning wasn't the goal of the physics class—at least not on this test. A *B* was good enough, so there wasn't any need to keep studying. (He got an 87, by the way…a solid *B*.)

This reminds me of a story Myron Dueck, author of *Grading Smarter, Not Harder,* told in an interview about his book (ASCD, 2014). He was frustrated with having to nag his young son about brushing his teeth each night, so he told him that he would start fining him a quarter every time he needed to be reminded to brush. His son said, "All right," and disappeared for a bit. Feeling a bit smug, Myron turned to his wife and said, "Hey…successful parent!" Then his son reappeared and slapped seven quarters down on the counter and said, "I'm good for the week." His wife looked at him and said, "Successful parent, eh?"

Both of these stories illustrate how incentives signal to students that learning or behavior are transactional. Instead of worrying about learning (in my son's case) or health (in Myron's son's case), grades and quarters drove the thinking. Transactional thinking pushes people down the moral reasoning and academic engagement hierarchies. Instead of leading to deeper engagement and self-motivation or higher-order ethical thinking, they place people's thinking in the "What's in it for me?" stage.

This phenomenon of transactional thinking lowering ethical behavior isn't confined to the world of children. Steven Levitt and Stephen Dubner share one such story in their book *Freakonomics*. A couple of economists were trying to help solve the problem of a day care center in Israel that was struggling with parents who were showing up late to pick up their children. In a carefully conducted study, which spanned 10 day care centers over 20 weeks, they implemented fines for late parents to try and incentivize them to show up on time. This fine did change parents' behavior, but not in the way they intended. It more than doubled the number of tardy pickups! Why? Instead of parents feeling obligated to show up on time—to respect the school and maintain relationships with teachers, not to mention to be responsible for their children—they were now thinking economically. As it turns out, many of them would gladly pay a bit more money for extra day care services. The fine removed their guilt about showing up late (2009, pp. 14–20).

One of the most frequently frustrating questions that middle school and high school kids ask is, "Is this going to be graded?" or "Is this on the test?" They have learned to view learning and schoolwork as transactional, except here, grades—not cash—are the currency. Have you ever noticed that younger children who haven't yet experienced grades don't ask these questions? Might this not indicate that grades, at least in part, are driving down feelings of engagement in students?

When we give students a rubric with points that add up to a grade, we shouldn't be surprised when they figure out how to get the number of points to get their desired grade (which might be an *A* or only a *D*) with the least amount of effort possible. When we offer students gems in a jar or stickers on a chart or school cash to be kind or polite or respectful, we should expect some kids to decide they don't really care about stickers or gems or school cash and therefore decide that they don't need to be kind, polite, or respectful. Or if they do care about these things, they might only display these behaviors when someone is around who might give them tokens. Without meaning to, we may crowd out higher-level engagement and moral reasoning with lower-level motivations while also signaling that engagement and ethical thinking are behaviors that aren't expected without compensation.

Unethical Behavior

In addition to lowering moral reasoning so that kids are acting more out of self-interest than we want, incentives can even encourage unethical behaviors such as lying, cheating, and stealing. Why do we have to be so careful about kids cheating on tests? Perhaps it's because getting a good grade crowds out real learning. Why might professional athletes pump themselves full of dangerous performance-enhancing drugs? Because a contract of $200 million will set their family up for financial security for generations. Why might rich parents lie and cheat to get their kids into elite colleges? Because the prestige of good schools is more important than how they get there. Why might business executives fudge quarterly reports? Because profit margins have outweighed ethical business practices. Even the time-honored tradition of offering bonuses for meeting goals in the workplace has been shown to increase employees' dishonesty (Sauer, Rodgers, & Becker, 2018).

Think back to the story of when my system of chips for pizza fell apart. Remember how some of my students were accusing each other of stealing chips out of each other's dishes? Now that I better understand some of the downsides of incentive systems, I wouldn't be surprised if some kids were actually stealing chips from other groups.

Carol Dweck encountered this discouraging phenomenon while researching children's mindsets about learning. One particular experiment was designed to uncover the connections between praising kids for their abilities ("You're so smart!"), which is a kind of verbal incentive (prestige is the reward), and their mindsets about learning. If you're familiar at all with the concept of a growth mindset and Dweck's work, then you won't be surprised to hear that this kind of ability-based praise led kids into a fixed mindset. They were more likely to avoid challenges and scored lower on spatial reasoning tests. Then, something shocking happened. Dweck explains:

> There was one more finding in our study that was striking and depressing at the same time. We said to each student: "You know, we're going to go to other schools, and I bet the kids in those schools would like to know about the problems." So we gave students a page to write out their thoughts, but we also left a space for them to write the scores they received on the problems. Would you believe that almost 40 percent of the ability-praised students *lied* about their scores? And always in one direction.... What's so alarming is that we took ordinary children and made them into liars, simply by telling them they were smart. (2006, p. 73)

So although we use extrinsic motivators to boost students' academic engagement and help them learn prosocial skills and attitudes, these systems might be driving students in the opposite directions.

Incentives Damage Relationships and Morale

Imagine that you've just accepted a new teaching position in a new school. You're meeting with your administrator for the first time since the interview, and you're eager to make a connection and start to build a positive relationship. You sit down in her office so she can run through a few things you should know about the school.

"I'm excited to share a new incentive system I'm implementing this year," she explains. "It's something we've never tried before, and I have a special grant through the state to fund it. Here's how it works. In order to encourage teachers to work hard and try and help kids learn, every quarter I'm going to hand out $1,000 bonus checks for teachers who are doing a good job. If you show up to work on time, put in lots of effort, and use the teaching programs and practices we're implementing as a district, you can earn up to an extra $4,000 a year. Isn't that exciting?"

How would you feel? On the one hand, you might be excited about the idea of an extra $4,000 a year. That's a significant amount of money and might mean the difference between needing a summer job or being able to focus on professional learning in July. On the other hand, your heart might sink a bit as well. Why?

Signaling: Distrust

Again, we return to the concept of signaling. When this kind of controlling motivator is used, it sends a message that the controller doesn't trust the receiver (Falk & Kosfeld, 2004). Being offered a reward signals that whoever is offering you the reward has a low opinion of your self-motivation. This feels demeaning, and your effort will likely drop (Frey & Jegen, 2001). After all, wouldn't you be somewhat offended by this? The reason you're going to work hard and teach well is for the benefit of your students and your eagerness to help them succeed. You might begin to wonder, doesn't your principal trust that you want to be a great teacher without needing extra motivation?

When we offer kids incentives for doing good work or behaving well, we may unintentionally signal to them that we don't trust them, which can damage the relationships we're trying to build with them.

Not surprisingly, negative incentives such as punitive consequences work the same way. Ross Greene makes a great point about how not getting a positive incentive still feels like a punishment to a child (2014), so from this perspective, any incentive system might be viewed as having a negative component. One study I examined found that when punishments are threatened, it leads to less trustworthy behavior—it's what the authors called one of the "hidden costs" of explicit punishment threats (Fehr & List, 2004). Interestingly, this same study indicated that when there was a clear availability to punish (like we see with the dynamic of teachers and students in a classroom) but threats aren't used, more trustworthy behavior was exhibited.

When kids feel they're not trusted, it can have a devastating effect on the climate of the classroom. Will students be willing to ask adults or other students for help if they don't feel relational trust? Will they be ready to take appropriate academic and social risks if they don't think they're trusted?

Competition

Incentives can sometimes encourage competition among students and pit them against one another. This is one of the downsides to traditional grading systems, where echoes of grading on a bell curve still persist. If teachers think that if all students get high grades in a class, they're not rigorous enough, they may design learning tasks and assessments to ensure that only a few students can excel. Grades aren't as much about mastering content as they are about mastering it more than your classmates. Similarly, when tests are scaled so that the highest grade becomes a 100 and all other grades slide upward accordingly, grades don't reflect mastery of content—just students' understanding as compared with the "top" student.

One teacher told me a story about how this same idea played out in his school in relation to a behavior management system. Teachers were all supposed to give kids tickets for good behavior. The tickets could then be traded in at the school store for merchandise. There was a stipulation in the system that backfired. Certain students who were very disruptive, identified by well-intentioned administrators and case managers, were supposed to get five positive pieces of feedback (tickets) for every correction they were given. The goal here was noble: to make sure struggling students were getting noticed for lots of positive things, not just hammered for their mistakes. This meant, however, that the students with the most dysregulated behaviors were the ones flush with cash at the school store. You can imagine how unfair this felt, and many students were confused and jealous.

If one of our intentions is to build a sense of positive community and personal relationships between students, the competitive nature of some incentives clearly is out of step. It's hard for students to feel a sense of collaboration with people with whom they are constantly competing.

Shaming

One spring evening, my daughter Carly was sitting on the floor by the woodstove, clearing out a school notebook and recycling old work. As she was removing tests, quizzes, homework assignments, and notes from a previous high school math class, she commented, "Ms. Cooper [a pseudonym] was a really great teacher. We did so many cool projects in that class. But she had this Super Sticker Board." "What was that about?" I asked. "If you got a 90 or above on a test or quiz, you got a sticker on your paper and your name went up on the Super Sticker Board. Everyone could see the names." Her eyes and voice dropped a bit as she continued, "I didn't have my name up there very much." Now, of course, Ms. Cooper had the best of intentions, and she most likely didn't know that her Super Sticker Board was stressing out my daughter (and others, I'm sure). She was clearly trying to motivate and celebrate, not realizing that, for some, this system was embarrassing. It was clear that even though my daughter did reasonably well in the class, she felt a bit of shame about not being on the board very often.

This is yet another downside to incentives. When students don't get the rewards, or when they're punished through negative incentives, they often experience humiliation and shame—emotions that make learning much harder. For children who are often right on the edge of fight, flight, or freeze and for students who struggle with emotional regulation, getting punished or not getting a reward can be emotionally devastating. Young children might cry or melt into a tantrum. Older students might become more emotionally distant or seek revenge. Ironically, it's often for these most challenged and challenging students that we try incentives in the first place. The kids who most need a sense of competence and emotional safety have these very needs undermined by the incentives we're using to try to help them.

Exacerbating Inequities

Here's another way incentives can harm the kids we're trying to support. I was working with a team of middle school teachers. They had a star incentive system they had been using for a while, and they were reluctant to give it up, even though it clearly wasn't working. (That is, after all, why we were working together—they were looking for help with kids struggling with responsibility and respect.) Before we go on, let's be clear. This team of teachers was an incredibly caring and dedicated group. They truly wanted to foster important skills and behaviors in their students.

Here was how the system worked. Every Monday, all students started off with five stars on a card. Every time they didn't bring a pencil to class, forgot their homework, didn't pay attention well enough, were disruptive, or displayed any other frustrating (though mostly developmentally normal) behaviors, they'd lose a star. At the end of the week, anyone who still had at least one star left got to enjoy a celebration of some kind (a special game, a movie, some extra outside time, etc.). Anyone who had lost all of their stars had to go to a study hall to make up the work they missed from being so irresponsible.

The teachers asked me what I thought of the system, so I asked them a few questions to help the group reflect.

Question: Is it working? Are students being more responsible and respectful?

Answer: It seemed to help at first, but it didn't last very long. After a few weeks, things kind of fizzled out.

Question: On Mondays, can you now accurately predict who will get the reward on Friday and who will be in the study hall?
Answer: Yes. It's pretty much the same kids, week after week.
Question: Are some kids now mocking the system? For example, are there some students who have made it into a game to see how quickly they can lose their stars on Monday?
Answer: Yes.
Question: And, as a general rule, are the kids who get the reward on Friday mostly from middle-class homes? Are the kids who are in the study hall, for the most part, children experiencing poverty?
Answer: Yes.

This last question and response reveal another problem with incentives, and it's heartbreaking, because so many educators care so deeply about equity. We want all students to have opportunities to be successful. And for many of us, helping children whose families are struggling is what gets us out of bed and off to school each day. We want to make a difference in those students' lives—to help them have lots of choices and opportunities as they grow up.

But if your school is using incentive systems that routinely reward kids from wealthy families and punish children experiencing poverty, a clear message is being sent: There are haves and have-nots in this school, and the have-nots can't be successful. We can't reward and punish our way to responsibility or kindness or self-regulation. Kids need direct instruction, modeling, and practice with skills and strategies to be successful. (We'll dig into this in depth in Chapter 5.)

FAQ: What about awards?

If it's the if-then nature of incentives that messes with motivation and achievement, does the same hold true for awards where the if-then component isn't as prominent?

Many schools have some kind of tradition of awards. Most high schools have honor rolls and award the title of valedictorian and salutatorian to the two seniors with the highest cumulative GPAs. Schools give perfect attendance awards at the end of the year or citizen of the week or month awards throughout the year. Some schools give a science scholar or math achievement award to students chosen by teachers as exemplary in a particular discipline.

Some research indicates that out-of-the-blue, unlooked-for rewards don't do the damage that if-then incentives do (Lepper et al., 1973). So if after an intense week of great work on a class project, you announce on a Friday afternoon, "Wow! We've put in such an amazing week of work! Let's celebrate with some games this afternoon," you're likely not doing any long-term damage. If the award is unexpected, little damage to motivation is done (Jensen, 1998, p. 66). If, however, you make this same declaration too often, it's going to start to feel like an if-then proposition for your students. I once heard a friend warn, "If you give your children dessert after dinner three nights in a row, it starts to feel like a right, not a privilege."

Consider the awards at your school. Are they routine enough that they feel expected? For example, if a Star Student of the Week award is given every Friday, no one has to explicitly say, "If you behave well, you might get chosen as a Star Student" for kids to see it as an incentive.

Another question to consider about awards in your school is "Why are we giving them?" It almost always has to do with incentivization or motivation. The answer might be "To celebrate the hard work and achievement of kids who go above and beyond," which sounds positive enough. But when you peel that back a bit, some troubling other messages emerge. If kids are putting in hard work and achieving at a high level, isn't their learning and achievement enough of a reward? If we say that the top students need some kind of tangible or public recognition, are we accidentally saying that learning and growth aren't enough motivation on their own? We may also signal to students who don't win the awards that their accomplishments and effort weren't worthy of pride or recognition. Because usually only a very select few students win these awards, we might consider the damaging messages being sent to the many other hardworking and accomplished students out there.

Conclusion

If systems of extrinsic motivation tend to undermine intrinsic motivation, diminish learning and performance, lower moral reasoning and academic engagement, and even damage relationships and morale, why are we still using them? If decades of research demonstrate the potential downsides to the broad use of incentive systems and multiple student surveys (not to mention our own experiences) show that student engagement and motivation drops over time as children progress through schools, why are these systems still so prevalent?

This is an important question that needs to be addressed before we start looking at the alternatives. If we don't understand why (and how) we get stuck in these systems, it's going to be really hard to break the cycle.

3

Why It Is So Hard to Let Go of Extrinsic Motivation

This is hardly the first book, and I am hardly the first author, to make the case that schools should move away from extrinsic rewards. Authors like Alfie Kohn (*Punished by Rewards: The Trouble with Gold Stars, Incentive Plans, A's, Praise, and Other Bribes,* 1993); Dan Pink (*Drive: The Surprising Truth About What Motivates Us,* 2009); Richard Curwin, Allen Mendler, and Brian Mendler (*Discipline with Dignity: How to Build Responsibility, Relationships, and Respect in Your Classroom,* 2018); and Dominique Smith, Douglas Fisher, and Nancy Frey (*Better Than Carrots or Sticks: Restorative Practices for Positive Classroom Management,* 2015) have all made compelling, clear, and widely read arguments against the use of extrinsic motivation.

Developmentalists like Jean Piaget, Arnold Gessell, and Chip Wood have offered parents and teachers incredible research and practical strategies for viewing growth and development through a maturational viewpoint: Development is predictable, and we should follow the child's lead (with guidance and support) instead of overdirecting and managing their development. Children flourish in Montessori and Reggio Emilia schools, where children lead the way and coconstruct the curriculum with teachers instead of using a rigid preconstructed model and forcing children to be compliant in it.

It's clear that there are many other—and better—ways of supporting students' motivation, so let's explore a few reasons why these systems that focus on extrinsic motivation seem to have such staying power.

Incentive Systems Are Familiar

Did you grow up in a system of carrots and sticks? Most of us probably did. Punishments and rewards motivated behavior, and stickers and grades motivated academic work. Chances are that most of us also felt pretty comfortable playing this type of school game. We knew how to do the work we were supposed to do, and we knew how to behave the way we were supposed to behave. (In fact, we may have felt so comfortable playing this school game that we decided to keep playing it as a career.)

Writer and researcher Dana Haight Cattani (2002) confirms this idea in her exploration of how new teachers develop professionally, *A Classroom of Her Own:*

> Those who go on and become teachers are often the kind of people who have led past lives of academic success and sufficient obedience to view school positively (Lindblad & Prieto, 1992; Schmidt & Knowles, 1995; Willower, 1969). Moreover, successful students with biases toward obedience are likely to be invested in the authority systems of schools.... Compliance may be a natural or rational choice to these prospective teachers. In either case, the kinds of students who go on to be teachers are more likely to be experienced in submitting to authority than in exercising it. (p. 6)

Incentives are familiar to our students as well. They've probably experienced them at school and at home. As a classroom teacher, each year in September I would develop class rules with my students—leading them through a process for establishing norms to guide our work and behavior throughout the year. As I would open a class discussion about ideas for respectful and reasonable consequences for common mistakes (blurting out during a lesson, leaving snack wrappers on a table, shoving in line, etc.), students would regularly suggest much harsher consequences than I was comfortable with. "If someone shoves someone else, they should have to come in for recess and sit with their head down on a table!" "If someone swears, they should have to write a letter of apology to the class and stand up and read it out loud!" "If someone runs in the hall, they should have to go to the principal's office!" Later in the year, when holding a class meeting to solve a class problem (such as people not returning supplies to supply bins), students would invariably suggest reward systems. "Last year we had a sticker system. Every time we did something good, we'd get a sticker, and when we got 10 stickers, we could skip a homework assignment!" Of course, students suggested ideas that matched their past experiences.

Incentive systems are also familiar to parents. Like teachers, most parents grew up with these systems, and many now use them at home. Teachers sometimes worry that parents will complain if they don't use some kind of incentive system. Teachers may also worry that administrators will think they don't have a structured classroom if they're not using a behavior chart or some other similar management system.

It's important to know, however, that these systems have only been around for a couple of generations. Developed by noted behaviorist B. F. Skinner, token economy systems were designed to support people—especially children—with extreme behavior challenges. Skinner did not design token economies to be used as a broad-based program for children in schools. He was very clear that most people have the self-control that make these types of systems unnecessary (Skinner, 1976). After a brief burst of popularity in institutions such as mental hospitals, juvenile detention centers, and prisons (Hare & Woods, 2013, p. 229), these systems faded from clinical settings. People were troubled by the morality of withholding privileges from mental patients and prisoners.

Interestingly, as these systems largely disappeared in clinical settings, they transitioned to widespread use in schools and homes, again, settings they were not initially designed for. Parents posted sticker charts on fridges, schools offered cash for turning in homework, and I used chips with the promise of pizza to control my students.

Incentives are now so ubiquitous in education that they just seem like they're supposed to be there. For example, in the spring of 2020,

Massachusetts spent a lot of energy encouraging its citizens to fill out the census. One of the TV ads took place in an elementary school classroom, and if you look closely, on the board in the back of class is a Math Star of the Week poster. Someone creating this commercial decided that the scene just wouldn't be complete without a reward system in the background. This is how these systems sometimes feel: It just wouldn't be school without them.

Incentives Seem to Work—At First

If you've ever implemented an incentive system—one based on rewards, punishments, or a combination of the two—you've seen how quickly they seem to work. When you mention the prospect of a pajama party, kids cheer. When you threaten to take away recess or students' phones, they snap into line quickly. This quick burst of better behavior is like a shot of espresso for the teacher—it's an immediate jolt of positive feedback. "Yes, it worked!" we think.

This initial success is enough to reinforce our misunderstanding that incentives work. I remember how proud I was when I first introduced my system of chips for pizza. When all I had to do was look at a student and pat my pocket (where the chips were) and they lowered their voice (and their eyes), I thought I was seeing evidence that the system worked. As the system unraveled a few months down the road, it happened so slowly that it was hard to see the connections between the eroding classroom culture and the use of rewards and punishments.

This can lead to a tough cycle to break. Fooled by the initial success of the incentive, we think, "The incentive worked earlier, so I need to do more of that." We double down and offer new or better incentives, which gives a new burst of short-term energy and success, followed by the inevitable decline, which leads to the next increase.

Incentive Systems Are Addictive

One of the greatest fears adults voice when debating a shift in grading based on points and compliance to one based on competence is about motivation. "Grades are such good motivators for some kids. Won't kids stop caring about work if the work isn't graded?" they argue. We might even say, "Grades worked for me. I was super motivated to get grades. I don't think I would have cared about work without them." These worries are completely justified once students' self-motivation has been crowded out by grades. And this is just what happens. As students progress through their school experience, they tend to move from self-motivation and engagement to compliance and disengagement. Here's how this unfolds over time in a school district.

In preschools and kindergartens, you'll see children happily getting to work each day as they enter school. They can't wait to draw, color, cut, act, sing, read, write, count, and play. They're engaged in learning for learning's sake because it's fun, purposeful, and joyful. Something is likely happening in these classrooms, however, that is sowing the seeds of disengagement in later grades. Children are being taught—slowly and almost imperceptibly—to refocus their attention, away from the joy of learning and to what their teacher wants them to do. For example, if a child builds a big tower of blocks, exhibiting perseverance and practicing engineering skills of weight distribution and balance, the teacher might say, "Tyson, you worked so hard on that tower! How did you get those blocks to balance so high?" This would reinforce Tyson's sense of mastery and connection with his teacher while helping him practice articulating his thinking. However, if what he hears instead is, "Great job! I love how you built that tower!" Tyson receives the message that pleasing the teacher seems to be the real goal in school. As he progresses through elementary school, he experiences sticker charts, Student of the Week awards, and lots more teacher-centric praise. Knowing what we now know about the negative effects of extrinsic motivators, we can predict what will happen. Tyson will gradually lose interest in schoolwork, coming to see learning as a series of exercises in compliance. He will become dependent on these systems for his motivation or he'll lose motivation for schoolwork altogether.

Then, at some point during elementary school or middle school, Tyson will start to experience grades—the next attempt to motivate him to care about work. And, again, after a short burst of enthusiasm, he'll likely either feel only motivation to get grades, or if he struggles academically, he may stop caring at all about his work. By the time he is well into middle school and high school, his intrinsic drives have been shoved way into the background. He either appears to be not motivated at all, or he only seems to be motivated to get grades. He's hooked.

And so are we, his teachers.

As we watch kids' motivation slowly fade over the years, and we continue to pour time, energy, and resources into praise, rewards, and grades, we feel like there are no other alternatives. "These kids just don't care!" we cry. "I need to find ways to motivate them!" Or we lament, "These kids only care about grades. They won't do any work unless it's graded!" It's like we're all hooked on coffee, and every time we come down off of the caffeine high, we see no alternative but to grab another cup of joe.

Incentives Offer a Façade of Control

Another reason incentives are so hard to get rid of is that they offer teachers the illusion of power and control. In the minds of many, having control of your class is one of the markers of a good teacher (e.g., "There is Ms. Hunter. She always has such great control of her students," we can hear a proud principal brag as she gives a tour of the school to a new family).

When I walked around the classroom tossing chips into dishes, it reinforced my sense of power and control. The same is true for controlling praise. When I'd roam the room, praising the littlest things kids are doing to reinforce that they were doing what I wanted ("I like the way you're working so quietly, Carradine!"), I was reinforcing the idea that I was in charge.

The same may be true for doling out punishments. When we give a student an *F* for not turning in an assignment (which is reflection of a behavior, not necessarily a lack of understanding), we again feel a sense of power. "At least I did something. Someone needs to hold these kids accountable. They need to learn that there are consequences for not doing what they're supposed to do," we rationalize. We think we're teaching responsibility, but what skills of responsibility have been taught? This feels a bit more like failing the child. It's like we've thrown a kid into the deep end of the pool, watched them drown, and then declared that we're teaching them to swim.

This is, perhaps, one of the things that is most troubling about these systems. Even when they're not working—when kids are still not doing work or are being rude or aggressive—these systems *feel* productive. By withholding a pizza party or by failing a student, the adults get the illusion that they're in control. "At least I'm doing something," we think.

We're Told to Use Incentives

One of the main reasons we continue to use incentive systems is that we're often told to do so.

New Teachers Are Encouraged to Use Them

Very often, new teachers are encouraged to use management systems that involve tokens and rewards as a way of having some initial control of a class. The assumption is that new teachers don't yet have more refined, nuanced, or well-developed management skills, so they'll need to rely on the carrot-and-stick approach to start. Novice teachers typically feel immense anxiety about handling challenging behaviors (Berkson, 2005), so they're eager for anything that may help. This is especially true when they don't have supportive induction experiences (Fry, 2007).

Though it may be true that new teachers don't have the experience of their more seasoned colleagues, I'm not so sure this means they are less capable of more complex or nuanced practices. I have seen plenty of new teachers with outstanding classroom management skills. Furthermore, I worry that by encouraging new teachers to use incentive systems early in their careers, we increase the chances that they'll continue to use them. Also, learning these strategies early in our careers sends a message that it's the teacher's job to manage kids' behavior instead of teaching them skills of self-management. We're trained to think with a "tips and tricks" mentality when it comes to classroom management. This means that even if we drop one form of incentive system, we're likely to pick up another, because we've been led to believe that this is what good management is all about—controlling kids' behavior. We bounce from one attempt to the next without realizing that the system of carrots and sticks is the problem.

School or District Mandates Require Them

Although it is generally agreed that meaningful school change takes time—and that schools shouldn't race for quick fixes—it's hard not to panic when you're a school or district considered in need of improvement. This is especially true when next year's funding is affected by this year's test scores. Incentive systems are quick and easy to implement, and they often yield immediate positive results. For districts who need to get better fast, it can be hard to resist the appeal of incentives.

If you work in schools in the United States, you've probably heard of Positive Behavioral Interventions and Supports (PBIS). It is a widely used framework for supporting good behavior and learning in schools, and it has many positive and powerful elements, such as teaching positive behaviors and an emphasis on schoolwide consistency. Interestingly, what they seem to be most known for is their advocacy of the use of extrinsic motivators in classrooms and schools. This seems to be a matter of debate, however. If you explore the PBIS website, you will indeed find resources that support the use of rewards (Horner & Goodman, 2009). On the other hand, a white paper published by The Center for Responsive Schools offers a different interpretation, explaining that "the PBIS framework emphasizes that schools should have methods for acknowledging students' positive behaviors but does not favor one type of acknowledgment over another, as long as the student clearly understands what specific behavior is being acknowledged" (Center for Responsive Schools, n.d., p. 7). So teachers might acknowledge positive behavior verbally ("That was a really kind deed when you helped Steven on the playground after he fell") instead of giving a token ("Good job helping a friend—here's a token for the school store!").

This nuance seems to be mostly lost on schools as they implement PBIS. Nearly everywhere I go, I see token economies as the primary vehicle for recognizing positive behavior in PBIS schools. Some teachers have even told me that these systems are being mandated at the state level.

This has all been exacerbated by the standards movement, which has pushed increasingly complex and abstract content into younger and younger grades. It is widely recognized that today's kindergarten classrooms often look and feel like 1st or even 2nd grade classrooms of 10 or 20 years ago. In his beautifully written book, *Reclaiming Childhood: Letting Children Be Children in Our Achievement-Oriented Society* (2003), William Crain explains the increased need for extrinsic motivation as schoolwork becomes more rote and less developmentally appropriate:

> As the standards movement presses forward, it constantly raises the issue of students' motivation—or, more accurately, students' lack of motivation. There is broad agreement, within and outside the standards movement, that students in traditional schools don't like their work very much and don't work very hard at it. But the standards movement doesn't call for more intrinsically interesting work—work that students find exciting and meaningful. Instead, the movement calls for more external pressures and incentives. Parents must push children to work harder for the sake of their future; states must threaten children with being held back if they don't perform well on standardized tests; and employers and colleges must let students know they will be rejected if they don't achieve high grades and high test scores in high school. Adults must be able to convince children that their schoolwork has real consequences. Otherwise, says economist and standards advocate James Rosenbaum, adults will be "like lion-tamers without a whip." (pp. 159–160)

Even if your school or district doesn't mandate these systems for all students, there's a good chance you might feel pressured to use them for specific students you work with. Incentive systems are often built right into individualized education programs (IEPs) for students receiving special education services. Although you might be compelled to go along with these systems for the sake of compliance with an IEP in the short term, it's worth opening up tough conversations about these systems with personnel in your school and district who help create these plans. Incentive systems do not have to be the go-to strategy to support children with challenges. Students would be much better off with plans that focused on setting realistic goals, leveraging intrinsic motivators (the topic of Chapter 4), and teaching students the self-management skills that they need to be successful (the topic of Chapter 5).

FAQ: Don't incentives help prepare kids for the world of work? After all, someday they're going to have a boss who's going to tell them what to do. If they don't do what they're told, they'll lose their job. Besides, people work for pay. Kids' job is to be in school, and grades are their pay. Isn't this the way the world works?

When you picture a typical work scene, you might envision a factory floor, where workers produce products under the watchful eye of a manager or supervisor. Or perhaps scenes from *The Office* appear. People sit at desks, sometimes working and sometimes goofing around, and a boss periodically pops in and either distracts or tries to motivate. In both scenes, we see the traditional role of management: to keep people on track and to motivate their behavior. We also see the traditional role of workers: to do what the boss says and to get work done.

In both of these scenes, intrinsic motivation is fairly low. If there's nothing inherently interesting about the work, why would workers care about doing much of it if they're not being compensated? In order to get people to assemble products more quickly or make more sales calls, their pay can be tied directly to their performance. Higher production should result in higher pay. Lower production should lead to a smaller paycheck or even result in a worker losing their job.

Now, we would hope that even workers in these straightforward jobs might feel some pride in a job well done and should care about high-quality work for the sake of quality. Or perhaps we hope that they feel investment in, and loyalty to, their company, so they see their work as part of a greater whole. But these things aren't really needed for rote formulaic work.

Similarly, in school settings, if the work is rote—if there isn't much to be self-motivated about—carrots and sticks are likely needed, and teachers will need to employ these techniques to make sure students stay on task. Again, we might hope that some kids will be self-motivated to do good work for the sake of good work, but this is likely more about compliance or gaining a sense of accomplishment based on teacher pleasing or parent pleasing than it is about true self-motivation.

There's an important aspect of this comparison that doesn't make sense, however. Traditional school reflects the world of industrial age work—but that's no longer what much of the modern workforce looks like, at least not in the United States and other developed economies. Factories have moved overseas. Computers and robots are replacing people doing jobs that are straightforward and rote. Many people telecommute at least one day a week, no longer working in a traditional workplace setting near their supervisors. Many U.S. workers now work for themselves as freelancers or telecommuters—they don't even have a boss—and need to manage and motivate themselves. In fact, according to a Forbes article, in 2017, about 57.3 million U.S. workers were freelancing, at least for part of their work—which translated to 36 percent of the workforce (Pofeldt, 2017). So if we want to help kids really be ready for the workforce, we should make sure they know how to motivate and manage themselves, not train them to be managed and motivated by others.

There are other problems with the comparison between kids in school and adults in the workforce. If you're stuck in a dead-end job, or you're unsatisfied with your working conditions or compensation, you can find a new job. As a kid, however, if you're unsatisfied with your school experience, you can't just switch 3rd grade classrooms or find a new school. If you're a high school junior, and you receive a teacher who brags about being an "evil grader" (a direct quote from one of my own children's high school teachers), you can't switch classes to find a better paying class.

What about the other part of this question? Doesn't money still motivate work? People wouldn't work if they weren't paid, right?

Absolutely. Few of us would or could work without getting paid. But, as you might at this point expect, money isn't always a motivator in the workplace in the simple and linear way we've been led to believe. This is something Dan Pink explores in *Drive* (2009). According to Pink's research, people need to be paid enough so that they're thinking about the work and not their pay. If you don't pay people enough, they won't be motivated. Once a fair wage is in place, autonomy, mastery, and purpose are much more important motivators in the modern economy. This is something teachers understand all too well. When we're underpaid—as compared to teachers in nearby communities or by the standards of the profession—we're demotivated. But pay isn't our primary motivation, and it never has been. I've never met a teacher who got into the profession because they're driven by money. (That would have been a bad move, wouldn't it?)

Conclusion

Now we're ready to dig into the solution. If we're not going to motivate kids with incentives, what will we do? And is it doable? By real human teachers?

As we'll see in the rest of this book, the alternative to the carrot-and-stick approach is more complex and nuanced. What makes the biggest impact for one student might be quite different from what another needs. We're going to need to think divergently, openly, expansively—not narrowly and concretely. We're going to need to be patient and steadfast and resist the allure of the quick fix. It's harder, but it's also absolutely doable and way better.

The first thing that we'll need to understand—and I mean really understand—is what the replacement is for extrinsic motivation. If kids aren't working for grades and stickers, if they're not behaving well to earn pizza parties or school cash, what are they working for? What will motivate them to engage in challenging schoolwork and act responsibly, respectfully, and ethically?

It's time to explore and understand six intrinsic motivators—motivators that we all share, and that we can cook into just about any learning activity for our students.

4

Understanding Intrinsic Motivation

In 2020, I had the privilege of participating in an online panel discussion hosted by Slate School in North Haven, Connecticut. The topic was "A Deep Dive into Learner-Centered Education." One of the other panelists was Maria Droujkova, the founding director of Natural Math. As she shared her thoughts as a part of the discussion, her hands never stopped moving. She was creating a paper snowflake using the host's name as the starting point. She kept talking about the beauty of mathematics and how even very young children can explore complex concepts when engaged in play and discovery. At one point in the conversation, she asked a powerful and important question: "What would children do if the door were open? Would they stay with us and keep doing what we were offering?" She went on to explain that this is a question for teachers to consider as we design learning activities for students. She continued, "How would you change the (learning) activity if you had voluntary clients?"

This question was particularly resonant considering the time and circumstances. In April 2020, nearly all children around the world were no longer physically in school due to the COVID-19 pandemic. In schools around the United States, teachers were suddenly struggling to get children to even participate in the most basic level of learning activities (Kurtz, 2020). Not only had the door opened, but the children had been forced to walk out and were now being encouraged to walk back in (albeit through a very different door). Many children decided not to come back.

Of course, there were a variety of reasons some kids didn't come back. Some didn't have access to technology or a reliable internet connection. Some had to shoulder extra burdens at home as their parents' work schedules changed, while others were helping care for family members who were sick. Some were homeless and didn't have a place to do schoolwork. But many children could have come back and didn't. Why didn't they? At least in part, it seems that the schoolwork itself wasn't meaningful or interesting, and without the usual confines and incentives of school, there wasn't much motivation to keep doing the work.

If we're going to let go of systems of extrinsic motivation, we need to keep Maria's important design question front and center. How do we make sure that students' work is so compelling that they are driven from within to accomplish it? That's the mission of the rest of this book: to uncover what to do instead of using systems of extrinsic motivation—because simply no longer using these systems isn't enough.

Instead of trying to motivate our students, we need to tap into their intrinsic motivations. We're going to explore six key intrinsic motivators that we can leverage to support students' motivation: autonomy, belonging, competence, purpose, fun, and curiosity. These six intrinsic motivators are fundamental and universal. They're not characteristics we need to teach but ones that all kids already have that we need to activate. They can help us craft learning experiences that are so engaging that kids will stay in the room, even if the door opens. In fact, I'd like to share a story about a time that kids weren't just willing to stay in school, they begged to come in—on a Saturday.

Timmy was worried, and I could see it in his eyes as he approached me toward the end of the day on Friday. "Mr. Anderson? Are you coming to school tomorrow?" I paused and replied, "Tomorrow's a Saturday. Do you mean Monday?" "No, I mean tomorrow. I know you come to school sometimes to do work on weekends. Are you coming to school tomorrow?" he pressed. Again, I paused. "I wasn't planning on it. Why?" His voice rose with anxiety—he was pleading now. "This model of Little Round Top is taking me so much longer than I thought it would, and I really need some more work time. Can I please come to school tomorrow to work on it?"

We were in the midst of a social studies unit called "Conflict in U.S. History." Every student was exploring a person or an event in American history that had some connection to conflict. Alyssa was studying Rosa Parks, Michael was studying the space race as a part of the Cold War, and Timmy was studying Joshua Lawrence Chamberlain and the 20th Maine Regiment from the Battle of Little Round Top from the Battle of Gettysburg. Students had spent several weeks researching topics, and they were now finishing up projects to use in their presentations, which were coming up next week. Timmy had put incredible time and energy into his work, but his vision of creating a model of Little Round Top (using balled up newspapers, masking tape, and papier-mâché) might have been a bit overly ambitious.

"Um, sure. I guess I could come in for a while in the morning. How about I be here from 8:00 to 12:00?" I ventured. "Yes! Thanks, Mr. A.!" Timmy practically skipped back to his work. Another student nearby had been listening. "Wait! Timmy's coming in tomorrow? I have a lot of work to do! Can I come in too?" A few other students nearby perked up and looked at me. So I made an announcement to the class: "OK, everyone. I know some of you would like some extra work time for your projects. I'll be here from 8:00 to 12:00 tomorrow morning. If you want to come in and get some work done, you may. I'll put together a quick note to your parents, so they know it's OK. Just to be clear—this is an extra work period, not an indoor recess. Only come in if you've got a lot of work to do."

The next morning, would you believe that 11 of 22 students showed up to work on their social studies research projects? Kids were incredibly productive, and it was clear that they loved the idea of being in school on a Saturday. We had a great time.

This was, by the way, a nongraded assignment.

Students had set some of their own goals, and we also had goals from the curriculum that everyone was working toward. Students had checklists to keep them on track, and I was engaged in almost nonstop conferences and coaching sessions with students to support their work. They had developed a real interest in their topics and investment in their work, and they were excited (and nervous) for their presentations. These presentations were a big deal. They ranged from 30 to 45 minutes, they had to connect with at least three of the Multiple Intelligences, and they had to be active and interactive. Kids played games, gave quizzes, and had classmates solve puzzles and engage in turn-and-talks.

This was also a class with incredibly diverse academic abilities and needs. Timmy was reading (with some support) college-level texts, and he was just one of several students who read way above grade level and had other skills that were quite advanced for 5th grade. Many students were right where you'd expect 5th graders to be, and several more really struggled with reading and other core skills. One in particular came in before school several days a week for extra reading support (from me and a volunteer tutor) because he was reading at about a 1st grade level. Another student had Down syndrome, and several others struggled (and I mean *really* struggled) with self-regulation due to trauma and chronic stress. They were a wonderful and very challenging group.

What was going on with this project? Why would so many 5th graders be so self-motivated that they were willing to (no—they begged to) come to school on a Saturday, especially without the traditional incentive of a grade? Keep that question in mind as you explore these six key intrinsic motivators.

Autonomy

power   control   self-discipline   influence   impact
effectance   liberty   ownership   origin of action
AUTONOMY
freedom   self-regulation   self-management
efficacy   empowerment   self-direction   impact

Have you ever watched a young child—a 1- or 2-year-old—start to seek autonomy? It can be amusing, frustrating, and even alarming as infants and toddlers start to experiment with power and control. At mealtime, they grab the spoon to try and feed themselves (increasing the length of mealtimes and the number of baths required to get sweet potato and applesauce out of their hair). Harvard professor and psychologist Robert White explained that young children would get more food by letting their parent feed them, but feeding themselves brings a different kind of satisfaction. As children learn to crawl and walk, they start experimenting with what they can do. They push open doors, rip books, throw food, and run in parking lots. White called this drive *effectance* "because its most characteristic feature is seen in the production of effects on the environment" (White, 1960). An episode from my own children's early years stands out as an example. Ethan, age 4, was "projecting." This meant he was constructing something—in this case it was a radio, made from a toilet paper tube and a pipe cleaner with buttons drawn with marker. Carly, age 2, was watching Ethan work, and you could sense that she was trying to figure out how she could have some kind of impact on the whole scene. She reached out, grabbed his radio, and held it, watching him. He immediately grew agitated: "Carya!" (his pronunciation of Carly) he cried. "Carya! Give it to me!" Carly stood, watching Ethan ramp up, and then, in one deft movement, she crushed the radio and threw it in front of him, watching (I assumed) in satisfaction, as he collapsed into tears. Aaah! The power!

The need for self-direction is fundamental and appears to be critical for intrinsic motivation. Richard Ryan and Edward Deci make the case that of all intrinsic motivators, autonomy might be the most crucial. They explain that even a sense of competence won't enhance intrinsic motivation without a sense of autonomy (2000). This means that if you're good at something, but you don't feel like you have some power and control in the situation, you still may not be motivated. This may help explain why some people can be good at their jobs or kids could be good at playing a musical instrument or a sport but still not enjoy it. If the job is one they felt like they didn't choose (e.g., "My parents wanted me to be an engineer") or the sport isn't one they wanted to play (e.g., "I was forced to play baseball"), they might be good at it but still not want to practice, play, or work on a project.

You can see now why autonomy is so important if we want kids to be truly motivated to learn. What if all students felt a sense of power and control over their learning? If students feel like they don't have any power and control over their schoolwork, intrinsic motivation might be impossible.

As you consider autonomy in your classroom or school, a helpful question to explore is "Who owns the work?" Do students have plenty of chances to make choices about what they learn or how they learn it, or is almost all of what they do dictated by others? Do students ask lots of questions, or do they spend far more time answering questions that others (teachers and textbooks) have asked? Do students set their own learning goals, or do the goals come from teachers or curricular guidelines?

Autonomy in Action

I was visiting a high school Spanish class in rural Maine. The class was approaching the end of a unit, and the teacher wanted everyone to have some time to consolidate learning before moving onto the next unit. I watched as she briefly described students' four choices—ones involving speaking, listening, reading, and writing. "You'll have about 40 minutes to work on your choices, and you should try to get to at least two of the options. Turn and talk with a partner—which ones do you think you should start with?" Students started sharing ideas with each other with animation and purpose, and when the teacher let them know they could start, they immediately got up and moved around the room to get the options they thought were best. The classroom had an industrious and purposeful tone as students engaged in a mix of activities.

Another example of autonomy can be seen in Jess Arrow's play-based kindergarten classroom at Symonds Elementary School in Keene, New Hampshire. For significant portions of each day, students get to engage in a wide range of possible choices as they work: building with blocks, engaging in dramatic play, looking at books, writing and drawing stories, and more. Just about everything that is on display in the classroom is fair game.

One day when I was visiting her classroom, she directed me to join a boy at a math table so he could share a game he had invented with me. This student gave me a lid to a small box and explained the rules of the game. When it's your turn, you roll two dice. Whatever number comes up, you take Cuisenaire rods (wooden rods with colors to indicate their length) in whatever combination you want that's equal to the number you rolled. You then place those inside the container lid. Your goal is to fill the inside of the lid without any gaps. We played several rounds of this game (with a couple of other students joining at one point), and I was amazed at the math concepts at work: counting, number sense, spatial reasoning, and number recognition were just a few.

What was most exciting for me was the immense pride this student felt in his game. He had already taught it to many other students in the class and had just made an appointment to teach students in the next-door kindergarten class as well. The freedom and flexibility students have in a play-based kindergarten is probably much closer to the working environment at Google than a high school computer science class where students are following directions to code a program with a predetermined outcome.

FAQ: I worry about giving my students too much control. What if I lose control?

It's important to balance power and control with students. It's not as much about *giving* kids control as it is *sharing* it with them—and we should only share as much as they can handle. Although our goal is to increase student independence and boost their sense of autonomy, we are the architects of the learning environment. You'll learn more about this balance as you explore Chapters 6, 7, and 8.

How Extrinsic Motivational Systems Can Diminish Autonomy

Let's briefly consider how systems that emphasize extrinsic motivation can mess with autonomy. When students are supposed to be working for marbles, stickers, grades, and other tangible items, who has the control? Although adults will often articulate to kids that this gives them the control ("It's your choice—you can choose your behavior to get what you want"), the control clearly sits with the one in charge of the system. It's usually the adults who decide what the tokens are, how students will earn them, and whether or what prizes are earned.

One of two things usually happens with kids' autonomy in these systems. They either give in to the system, abdicating their own power and control, or they refuse to submit. If they give in, they play the school game, figuring out what they need to do to get what they want, thus relinquishing their autonomy. If they refuse to submit, they resist—sometimes subtly, sometimes flagrantly and with defiance.

Belonging

affiliation   connectedness   relationship   connection   love
relatedness   personal significance   community   kinship
BELONGING
friendship   relationship   inclusion   rapport
association   attachment   cultural relevancy

You're introducing an activity to a group. As you give directions and explain goals, a hand shoots up. "Are we going to get to work with partners?" "Yes, but..." you begin, but that's all students need to hear. They're suddenly eyeballing each other from across the room, whispering frantically to get the attention of friends, and gesticulating wildly—flapping their hands and motioning to each other to get closer. What's going on? What's the sudden panic all about?

Although Deci and Ryan argue that autonomy is the most important intrinsic motivator, Abraham Maslow might disagree. In Maslow's theory of human motivation (1943), belonging—the need for connection and affiliation—comes just after our most basic physical needs for food, water, shelter, and safety. We see this need in students all day long as they jockey for position in line to be next to friends, engage in side conversations, congregate in small groups for lunch in the cafeteria, and sneak peeks at social media sites when they should be working.

You may have felt the same frantic need as your students at times as a professional. Have you gone to a conference and scanned the crowd in the dining area, desperate to find a friendly face you can join for lunch? Have you felt the joy of connecting with colleagues for a happy hour after school on Friday or the excitement of working with a team of colleagues designing a curricular unit? The level of connection colleagues feel for each other, for better or worse, is often directly connected with how happy teachers are at school. When you know you have colleagues who are friends—people you can count on for a laugh or a hug—it makes all of the other daily challenges bearable. No matter how much you love your students and the content you teach, if you don't have strong connections with colleagues, it's hard to enjoy going to school each day.

Our challenge, then, is to make belonging an essential part of students' daily experience at school. We must create communities of learners who can work effectively with each other and give many small moments throughout daily work for kids to connect positively with each other.

Let's also not forget the importance of students feeling connection to teachers. You've likely heard the old adage, "Kids don't care what you know until they know that you care." When kids trust their teachers and feel a strong sense of connection with them, incredible learning can happen. I've seen this both as a teacher and as a parent. My own two children both have had incredible energy for schoolwork from elementary school right through college when they felt connected with their teachers. And when they think their teachers don't know them or care about them, they struggle to muster motivation for the content.

Belonging in Action

I taught one group of 5th graders that was particularly challenging. One of the students was the toughest I ever had—quick to anger, quick to melt down, and full of inappropriate sexual knowledge that seemed to burst forth quietly to other children as soon as I was out of earshot. He was the toughest, but he wasn't the only challenging student in that class. Several were reading so far below their peers that it was hard to find high-interest books they could handle. There were other behavior challenges as well—students who could be defiant, argumentative, and sneaky. It was a class that demanded really good academic work—anything that hinted of being "boring" or "dumb" resulted in immediate disengagement.

One highlight that year was the movie we made as a class. I had planned on showing them just a short snippet of the Ken Burns documentary *Lewis & Clark: The Journey of the Corps of Discovery* to give them a brief taste of the era of Westward Expansion, one of our social studies units that year. I was hoping they could endure 30 minutes of the film, because I was sure that the slow pace, languid narration, and folksy banjo music would be a turn-off for this easily bored and distracted group. After 30 minutes, I paused the film to begin a brief class discussion, and they revolted. "Hey! Keep it playing! This is awesome!" We proceeded to watch the rest of the four-hour documentary over the next few days, and at the end, students suggested we make our own version.

For the next several weeks, we dove into the production. Small teams of students wrote scripts for various scenes. We created vast sweeping murals of the Rocky Mountains, Fort Mandan, the Pacific Ocean, and other key locations to use as background scenery. Students made makeshift costumes and props out of anything we could find around the school. They wrote, read, memorized lines, practiced, choreographed, filmed, and alternately bickered and collapsed into tears of laughter. In the end, we produced our own 30-minute documentary. They were so proud to show the movie to other classes and to their families and friends at an evening celebration in our classroom.

Clearly, more than one intrinsic motivator was in action here, but the overwhelming feeling of the project was one of togetherness. Students chatted happily as they colored in scenes with crayons on 12-foot-long sheets of butcher paper. They encouraged each other to practice lines and got each other to stay in for extra recesses and get to school early to keep working on the project. They felt a collective sense of responsibility to the project and accomplishment when the film was complete.

Seven years later, I was observing in a high school English class in that same district, and when several of those students—now seniors in high school—came into the room and saw me, the first thing they talked about was that project. "Do you remember when we kept laughing and couldn't talk?" "Do you remember when Anna had to pretend to be Sacagawea and had to give birth?" "Do you remember when Phillip had to die?" "Do you remember…" "Do you remember…" Seven years later, they still felt a sense of connection to each other when talking about that event.

FAQ: Should kids always work together?

No. Broccoli is a healthy food, but that doesn't mean we should eat it with every meal. There are times when students should work on their own. There are also times when we should offer students the choice of whether to work alone or with others.

In *Quiet: The Power of Introverts in a World That Won't Stop Talking,* Susan Cain (2013) makes a compelling case for how we have swung too far in the direction of collaborative work in schools, neglecting introverts' needs for self-reflection and solo work time. Also consider that kids can feel a sense of belonging without working collaboratively. Students reading independently can feel connected with friends as they read next to each other, hunkered down in beanbag chairs, even if they're reading different books and not talking.

FAQ: I want to do more collaborative work, but my students spend too much time fooling around or in conflict. What do I do?

Working with others is hard—often harder than doing work on your own. We need to teach students skills of collaboration: how to listen to each other, share ideas, disagree respectfully, divide work and roles equitably, and so on. These skills, which are keys to success both in school and out of school, need direct instruction, modeling, practice, and coaching, just like academic skills do. Collaborative work may be more challenging to manage at times, but it offers the perfect opportunity to help students learn key skills that they'll use long after the need to know the details of the Louisiana Purchase has faded.

How Extrinsic Motivational Systems Can Diminish Belonging

While we're trying to build collaborative and connected groups of students, motivational systems often encourage competition among students. Public discipline systems, such as clip charts, display for everyone to see who is winning and who is losing at the discipline game. Systems where the whole class wins or loses together often elicit peer pressure that erodes community membership. (Picture the scene after Jimmy has forgotten his homework once again: "Great, Jimmy! Thanks a lot! Now we're never going to get an extra recess!")

Traditional grades encourage kids to compete with each other. "What did you get?" is a common whispered question among students after a quiz is passed back. Some teachers throw gas on this fire by passing back tests in the order of grades received, or they highlight students who achieve at a certain level on a Star Student bulletin board.

We can appreciate how damaging these systems are to relationships when we think of the fallout they would cause if used with teachers. Imagine the humiliation of having to trudge to the front of a faculty meeting to clip down after you engaged in a brief side conversation. Imagine how unprofessional it would feel if performance reviews were passed back from worst to best in front of your colleagues. You may have felt a twinge of resentment as a colleague received a Teacher of the Year award when you think you also could have been recognized. Remember, it's hard to be collaborative and competitive at the same time.

Competence

mastery	achievement	growth	esteem	challenge
accomplishment	progression	success	ability	knowledge
		COMPETENCE		
know-how	proficiency	prowess	skill	inner strength
understanding	self-confidence	self-image	self-assurance	

Back in the early 2000s, I was struggling with health and balance as a teacher. With young children at home and students who had incredible challenges at school, I burned the candle at both ends—trying to summon superhuman strength and energy to do everything I thought I was supposed to do. Not surprisingly, I started to burn out. I didn't teach with as much fire as I wanted, and I was exhausted when I got home, so I didn't have the energy I wanted to have as a father either. Something needed to change, so I embarked on a research study to figure out how to better gain a sense of personal and professional health and balance. Throughout this research, I explored several categories of health and balance, and one rose to the surface as being surprisingly important (once you get beyond the most basic needs of sleep, healthy food, exercise, and hydration). It was competence.

Through reading many books and articles about workplace health and happiness, as well as talking with many teachers and engaging in important self-reflection, it became clear that without a sense of competence, it's almost impossible to be satisfied at work. You can earn a great salary, have great colleagues, enjoy good benefits, and have a wonderful physical environment in which to work, but if you don't think you're good at what you do or you don't see a viable pathway for getting better, you will eventually burn out (Anderson, 2010, pp. 67–68).

Have you seen this to be true in your own life? Do you find that you're motivated to do things when you're good at them or when you see yourself growing and getting better? Do you find it hard to be motivated to work at something when you feel incompetent?

Have you also seen this to be true with your students? Kids can pour their hearts and souls into something when they're good at it—when it delivers a sense of competence and esteem. Yet the very kids who need to pour their hearts and souls into work struggle to do so because they feel such a crushing weight of incompetence.

Robert White seems to be the first to name competence as a fundamental human need, in his eye-opening paper "Motivation Reconsidered: The Concept of Competence" (1959). Since then, this idea has gained widespread recognition. Edward Deci devotes an entire chapter to the topic in *Why We Do What We Do: Understanding Self-Motivation* (1995). Building on Deci and Ryan's work with self-determination theory, Dan Pink also extols the virtue of this motivator in *Drive*. He calls it *mastery* and defines it as "the desire to get better and better at something that matters." He goes on to explain that the pursuit of mastery is one of the most fundamental drives that "has become essential in making one's way in today's economy" (2009, p. 111).

I would also argue that there are important connections between competence and Carol Dweck's work on helping people develop a growth mindset. The basic premise of her work is that people are hardwired to be learners—to continue to grow our skills, talents, and intelligence—but if we develop a fixed mindset, we lose this desire to develop our competence (2006).

When we tap into students' need for competence—the desire to grow, learn, take on challenges, and master skills and content—it's incredible how motivated they can become.

Competence in Action

One teacher I was working with in Maine was teaching a calculus class. With only five students in the school ready for Calculus II, this was actually a Calculus I & II combination class—which meant that she had to differentiate content for her students. Her goal was to do so by letting her students choose appropriately challenging content—so that they were in charge (there's autonomy showing up again!) of self-differentiating their work. Just to make this scene as complicated as possible for you as a reader, in this particular class, they were practicing solving differential equations, so they were engaged in self-differentiating their differential equations. Is your head spinning yet?

She created a simple 5 x 5 grid with a problem in each box. The grid was colored so that it was dark blue in the bottom left corner and got pinker and pinker as you moved up and to the right. She explained the challenge to her students: "Try to find the problems that give you the just-right challenge level—ones that are hard enough to make you sweat a bit, but they're not impossible. If you start with one problem and it's too easy, go pinker. If you try one and it's too tough, go bluer. You've got about 25 minutes. Let me know how I can help. A heads-up…the top row of problems involves skills that only students in Calculus II have been practicing."

Her students were enthusiastic and clearly enjoyed the challenge of problems that were "tough enough to make you sweat." You can imagine how this same worksheet could have had a very different feel, can't you? She could have said, "You have 25 minutes to complete this worksheet. Start with the first one and work your way through. Be careful—they get harder as you go." An introduction like this would have made the task one of compliance instead of engagement and would transmit the idea that challenges are things to worry about rather than to relish.

FAQ: I did everything I could to set my students up for success, but they still didn't seem motivated. What's going on?

We must be careful not to create learning experiences for kids with no risk of failure. If all students need to do is follow the directions they're given and do as they're told to meet with success, there's no challenge. Kids will experience learning as an act of compliance or obedience and likely be bored. This is all about differentiated learning—helping students land in their just-right or "Goldilocks" zone, where work isn't too easy or too hard, but it's juuust right.

So we shouldn't "do everything we can to set students up for success," but we also shouldn't set them up for failure and leave them hanging out to dry. Our role as learning facilitators is complex. We need to help students set goals and take on tasks that are appropriately challenging, let them struggle, and also provide a guiding hand and a safety net to help them when they stumble. It's a bit like helping a toddler learn to walk. You provide the opportunity (a flat safe space without toys in the way), help them get a steady start (holding their hands as they begin), give them a challenging goal (a five-foot distance to cover to the next person), let them go, and be ready to help them get back up when they fall.

How Extrinsic Motivational Systems Can Diminish Students' Sense of Competence

Here are a few examples of how extrinsic motivators can diminish students' sense of competence.

- **Reward systems.** The motivational systems that reward students who are successful and punish kids who aren't demotivate the very kids who most need a sense of inner strength and self-assurance, as their notion that they're incompetent is reinforced.
- **Traditional grades.** The A–F grading system, whether or not it's still being implemented on a bell curve, encourages kids to compare how they did to how others did. For students who struggle with learning

and see themselves getting lower grades than their peers, this further reinforces the idea that they don't measure up.

- **False or shallow praise.** Meant to motivate, praise often has the reverse effect on students. When the praise sounds forced or inauthentic, kids get the idea that they must be incompetent—otherwise people wouldn't be trying to boost them up with fake praise.
- **Teacher-pleasing praise.** When teachers use phrases such as "I love the way you..." or "I like how you..." to give positive feedback, students may come to rely on teachers for knowing whether they've been successful. Their ability to accurately self-assess and feel good about their work for its own sake is replaced by their need to please others. Their self-worth can become dependent on the approval of others.

Purpose

meaning	significance	reason	aspiration
intent	function	desire	
	PURPOSE		
direction	ambition	connection	
rationale	context	value	determination

Some teachers don't like it when students ask, "Why do we have to do this?" Perhaps it's the tone that often accompanies the question—annoyance mixed with a twinge of desperation. Perhaps it feels threatening—as if the student has directly challenged the teacher, implying, "This is stupid, and I don't see the point!"

Personally, I love this question. I even encourage it.

As a classroom teacher, I would challenge my students to ask this question whenever they were unclear about why we were doing something. I also made a commitment to them: If I couldn't answer the question well—if I didn't have a compelling reason—we'd stop.

Our sense of purpose is a critical motivator. Unless we want blind compliance or obedience, it's important that students know why they're doing whatever kind of work is before them. And when there's a compelling reason behind work, students' motivation can go through the roof.

In his revolutionary book *Start with Why,* Simon Sinek (2009) explains how great leaders and great organizations (Martin Luther King Jr., Apple, and the Wright Brothers are just a few) are transformational because they know and can articulate their purpose—their *why.* This is incredibly important. As comedian and speaker Michael Jr. says, "When you know your why, your what becomes more impactful, because you are walking towards or in your purpose" (2017).

When we—teachers and students—work from a sense of purpose, our work can be so much more inspired. Too often in schools, purpose is defined in adult-centric terms, usually in some form of "You'll need this someday." You know what I mean:

- "Your 6th grade teachers are going to expect you to know your math facts, so you should learn them now."
- "Colleges expect students to be able to write a well-crafted essay."
- "If you're going to be successful with a job someday, you'll need to learn some responsibility."

Or some vague "other people" are the purpose for learning something. "It's part of the curriculum" or "It's on the state test we take in the spring" or "The program we use says we need to do this" are all versions of this kind of rationale.

For kids who most struggle with motivation, these abstract purposes don't resonate. Instead, we need to find more immediately relevant and compelling reasons for students to care about work. We can write letters (and actually send them) about things kids really care about. We can create bulletin board displays or put on presentations to share what we're learning with the rest of the school or our families. We can write and publish real stories and read and share about real books, not snippets of stories cobbled together in anthologies. When the work is real—from the perspective of the students—kids will dig in with incredible energy.

Purpose in Action

Holly was often belligerent, stubborn, uncooperative, and resistant to almost all schoolwork. She routinely folded her arms across her chest and glared at me when I tried to help her, spitting out her favorite disdainful refrain: "This is so *stupid!*" Schoolwork often felt pointless to Holly, and her academic and social struggles made her feel incompetent and lonely. She struggled with nearly all aspects of school: reading, writing, math, making friends, and just about everything else.

Desperate for something—anything—that would help her engage positively in school, I took a chance and reached out to a colleague of mine in 1st grade. I thought that if Holly could have the chance to work with a younger child who was also struggling, perhaps she'd rise to the occasion. And did she! When she had the chance to be a reading tutor for a 1st grader, her whole demeanor changed. She was sweet, gentle, persistent, and kind. She got more actual reading practice from reading to younger children than she did during our own 5th grade class.

There were several factors at work here. She had opportunities for competence and connection, but most importantly, I think this work felt real and genuine. The 1st grader she tutored really did need help, and Holly could provide it. This work had genuine purpose from Holly's perspective.

Here's another example. Pat Ganz's English class was made up primarily of sophomores who were reluctant learners, and he was searching for a way to help them feel a greater sense of urgency for their work. He contacted the nearby elementary school and asked if there was a classroom he could connect with. His students were arranged in small groups, and each group was paired with a small group of 5th graders. The high schoolers went to the 5th grade class and met with their buddy groups, interviewing them to find out their favorite foods, the music they liked, the sports they played, and other interests. Then, they took that information back to class and wrote short fictional stories where the 5th graders were the main characters, and their interests were featured in the stories. A few weeks later, they returned and read their stories aloud to their groups. Pat shared that this was the most motivated his students were that semester.

FAQ: What if I can't come up with a good answer to "Why do we have to do this?"

Sometimes, we may struggle with knowing why people need to know the Pythagorean theorem or understand the Wilmot Proviso. Or we might not believe in the amount of time spent (wasted?!) preparing for standardized tests. Our own sense of purpose might be lacking with some of the content we're required to teach. This is a time to manufacture some purpose through meaningful tasks. Perhaps students could create a class-produced game show to practice questions that might be on a state test. Or we might have the class design a bulletin board of examples of the Pythagorean theorem in the world around them. Building projects to share with others can lend a sense of purpose to many different topics in many content areas.

How Extrinsic Motivational Systems Can Diminish Students' Sense of Purpose

When I ask teachers what they hope drives student motivation, "a love of learning" is often the first answer given. Don't we all want students to see learning as the ultimate goal? Don't we want students to value learning and growth over all else?

When we redirect students' attention away from learning and toward grades, they often lose sight of the learning itself. This is where crowding out comes into play. It's hard to be motivated both by a sense of authentic purpose and by grades or other extrinsic motivators. So students typically land in one of two places. They either don't care about grades, so they don't care about the work (because they're being told that grades are the purpose), or they shift their purpose and focus primarily on getting the grades they want. They become fixated on grades—caring less about the work itself and only doing what they think they need to do to get the grade. The work has become a means to an end.

An elementary school principal recently told me that, even though her students don't receive grades, their motivation still drops as students get older. In her school, it's about praise. As teachers lavish praise on students ("I love the way you're working so hard!" "I like the way you added so much detail to your story!" "You're so smart in math! Look how fast you solved those problems!"), students' purpose shifts from learning to teacher pleasing. They understand that they gain approval and love by pleasing teachers, and this, just like grades, can undermine their intrinsic sense of purpose for work.

This shifting of purpose can also lead to cheating and other unethical behavior. One high school student told me of a classmate who would always ask her friends for their assignments so she could copy them, or ask about tests they had taken that she was about to take to look for the questions and answers ahead of time. The student graduated third in her class at a highly competitive high school and was furious she wasn't second. For her, grades seemed to be all that mattered about school.

Fun

	joy	pleasure	play	amusement
recreation	gratification		enjoyment	playfulness
		FUN		
	humor	state of flow	jollification	

Mark Twain once said, "Work consists of whatever a body is obliged to do. Play consists of whatever a body is not obliged to do." As much as I enjoy this quote, and as much as it may speak to a certain level of truth, I don't entirely buy it. Certainly, when you feel like you're being forced to do something, it's hard to feel like you're having fun. However, I also know it's possible to have fun even when engaged in something you're obliged to do. For example, I've been to professional development sessions that have been mandated by my district, and in fact, I've dreaded going, but once I get there and get going, I end up enjoying myself.

The same can certainly be true for students. They have to come to school, and there are certain units they need to explore and learning activities they need to do, yet there are still ways to bring a little joy and levity to the work. Children seek fun in the same way they seek belonging and safety. In fact, humans are programmed to learn through play, something that theorists like Vygotsky (1978) and Piaget (1946/1962) noted decades ago. More current research bears out the positive impact of play. Play helps children build skills of social competence and confidence (Golinkoff, Hirsh-Pasek, & Singer, 2006), and it also supports language development, literacy skills, and self-regulation (Guirguis, 2018). In a review of 70 studies, John Hattie determined that play programs had an overall beneficial impact on student achievement, which placed this strategy solidly in the "zone of desired effects" category of his synthesis (2009, pp. 154–155).

Unfortunately, fun has been a casualty of the standards movement. As pressure increased and accountability felt more burdensome, many teachers felt compelled to give up learning activities like class plays, cooking projects, moviemaking, hands-on projects, and using manipulatives in mathematics. After all, these things often take more time, and for some of them, even if we knew there was good learning in there, they might not have been directly linked to standards or clear learning goals. (I remember early in my career doing cooking projects and figuring, "There's measurement and fractions in there, kind of.") As we were handed more and more scripted units and curricula, carving out time for work that was fun felt unrealistic and even irresponsible.

Our challenge in schools today is to make sure the learning is fun *and* directly tied to curricular goals and objectives. There are two ways we might consider fun as a motivator. The first is that it can be a by-product of other motivators. Appropriately challenging tasks can be fun. Working with others and feeling a sense of belonging can be fun. When we craft learning opportunities that tap into some of the other intrinsic motivators, the learning can feel more enjoyable for students.

The second is to find ways to embed playfulness and energy into learning in ways that don't necessarily connect with other motivators. For example, students who are practicing long division might have three options. They can either solve problems you give to them, create their own problems to solve, or roll dice to determine the numbers to use in problems they build and solve. Offering choice and the opportunity to build their own problems can tap into students' needs for autonomy and competence. Rolling dice can add an element of chance and a gamelike quality that adds a bit of fun.

Fun in Action

Like most teachers in the spring of 2020, Trisha Hall, a 3rd grade teacher, was looking for something—anything—to engage her students after school shut down and learning moved online. She found a simple app that made a world of difference. The app allows you to get a picture of an animal and then record yourself talking. The app then plays your voice recording (in one of several goofy voice options) while making it look like the animal is talking. (Yes, its mouth actually moves.) She started off by having her terrier, Auggie, make announcements, give directions, tell stories, and say the Pledge of Allegiance. Students, of course, loved this and started sending her pictures of their cats, dogs, rabbits, and other pets for her to use. She then used students' pets almost every day as a part of her online teaching. This small simple strategy made a profound impact on students' engagement.

A high school physics teacher was looking for ways to help breathe some life and energy into students' learning about laws of motion, energy, and gravity. The textbook she had on hand had good information, but it was written in a dry and unengaging way. She created a challenge where students were given the textbook and some time to review the laws of motion, energy, and gravity they were learning about—just enough to gain some familiarity with them. Then, small groups of students were each given a link to a cartoon episode featuring Wile E. Coyote and the Road Runner. Each group had a designated amount of time to document as many ways these laws were broken as they could. Groups then shared their findings with the class—watching the cartoons and pausing to point out violations of the laws of physics.

Again, we see here several intrinsic motivators in action. This is an appropriately challenging task for high school physics students, so students' need for competence is satisfied. There's the potential for belonging as students work together, and they may also feel a sense of purpose as they prepare to share their learning with others. But there's no doubt that the addition of Road Runner and Coyote cartoons adds a bit of fun to the work as well!

FAQ: Does school always have to be fun? Must we try to turn everything into a game?

Goodness gracious, no. Fun is just one of the six intrinsic motivators we can tap into to create learning experiences that enable kids' self-motivation to shine through. Sometimes learning won't be fun. Instead, we might tap into belonging or purpose or competence. On the other hand, if we can make learning more fun, why wouldn't we?

How Extrinsic Motivational Systems Can Diminish Students' Sense of Fun

Interestingly, we sometimes use extrinsic motivational systems to try to make work feel more fun for kids. For example, we might offer kids stickers on a chart for every assignment they turn in, and when they get to a certain number of stickers, they can pick a prize out of a prize box. Fun, right? Or we might say to students, "OK, everyone, if you can work really hard for the next 30 minutes, we'll play a fun game at the end of class!" Shouldn't that build enthusiasm?

It does, but probably not in the way we want.

Here we see signaling at work again. When we tell students that if they work hard, they'll earn something fun, we're signaling that the work itself *isn't* fun. After all, if the work itself was fun, we wouldn't need to entice students with something else to do it. In fact, we have now positioned their assignment as a barrier to fun—a hurdle they have to overcome if they want to do something enjoyable.

Curiosity

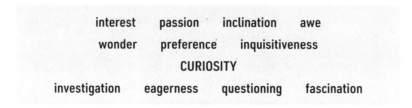

Is there something you've always been fascinated by—some quirky interest that you can't explain? One of mine is weather. I remember sitting at my bedroom window as a kid in Maine, watching snowstorms, mesmerized by the swirling and dancing sheets of snow. The dark pine tree across the street enhanced the visual image. For a while as a young adult, I kept a weather journal, noting observations and the high and low temperatures for each day, and I now have a weather station in my backyard that connects with the Weather Underground app (www.wunderground.com). When I make breakfast in the morning, The Weather Channel is almost always on in the background. I love to see what the weather will be like where I now live in New Hampshire, and I'm also fascinated by a tornado outbreak in Missouri, a typhoon hitting the Philippines, and a blizzard in Montana.

When you have an interest like this, you can be incredibly motivated, even in the absence of some of the other motivators such as purpose, belonging, and fun. My senior year in high school, I took a meteorology class as an elective. The teacher was a nice guy, but he didn't really know much about meteorology. He assigned chapters from a textbook and gave low-level quizzes and tests. The other kids in the class had no interest in the weather—this was a blow-off science class for them, and many of them sat on the tops of their desks socializing through most of class. I was still motivated to learn the content. I read the textbook, asked the teacher lots of questions (often eliciting a sheepish grin and a shrug), and did really well on tests (which weren't that hard, to be sure). I contemplated going into meteorology as a career, and if I hadn't found an even greater calling for working with children, I might have done so.

In his insightful and practical book *Out of Curiosity,* Bryan Goodwin digs into the topic of curiosity in great depth. In addition to making the convincing case that curiosity is hardwired into our species, he also points to import benefits of curiosity. Here are just a few (2018, p. ix):

- The more curious people are, the more they learn.
- Curiosity is more strongly linked to student success than IQ.
- In the workplace, employee curiosity and engagement are strongly linked.
- People who report greater curiosity report greater levels of happiness and life fulfillment.

He also sounds an important warning. Typically, the older children get and the more school they experience, the less curious they become. (Sound familiar? Remember how we earlier explored how creativity also drops as children get older?) While toddlers ask up to 100 questions a day, by the time these same children reach middle school, they may ask close to zero (Goodwin, 2018, p. x). It's hard not to wonder if this is a direct result of school. As children get older, do they see school as a place that feeds curiosity and wonder, or is it a place that's more about compliance? Do they spend more time asking questions and seeking answers to their own curiosities, or do they spend most of their time answering questions that others have formulated—ones that may or may not feel personally relevant? Without meaning to, do we guide students away from their interests and passions?

I remember one 5th grader, Aaron, who loved turtles. At open house night in the fall, I shared with families about how students would get to take on several independent research projects throughout the year—some of which would be focused on curricular themes, while at least one would be open-ended. Aaron's mother came up to me later and said she loved hearing about the research projects, "but please," she begged, "no more turtles! Aaron only wants to read and study about turtles, and I don't think I can take another turtle project!"

I laughed along with her and told her that I would not tell Aaron he couldn't study turtles, though I would make sure he was asking new questions and learning new information and new research skills. I told her about a lecture I'd attended recently at the University of New Hampshire by naturalist and author David Carroll, who discovered an interest in turtles when he was 8 years old. This led to a lifelong pursuit of observing, studying, drawing, and painting turtles. His memoir, *Self-Portrait with Turtles,* documents this incredible journey. He has spent decades studying turtles and turned his curiosity into a lifelong passion that has led to a fulfilling career.

There's an important side benefit for teachers when students are curious—our work is so much more engaging! When students' interests, passions, and curiosities are a part of the daily learning of the class, no two years will ever be the same, and we get to keep learning right along with our students!

Curiosity in Action

One of my favorite things to do with students is facilitate independent research projects—where students get to dig into content they're curious about. In fact, this was the topic of the first book I wrote, 15 years ago, with my friend and colleague Andy Dousis: *The Research-Ready Classroom* (2006). Research projects centered around science or social studies themes are worthwhile and exciting, but it's the open-ended ones—where students have more leeway to choose interesting topics—that are especially incredible. Of course, open-ended topics can still connect to whole-class competencies and skills such as speaking and listening, organization, nonfiction writing, and so much more. Here is one example that stands out.

Robby's older sister was taking a sign language class at the high school, and he became interested. He learned about the history of Thomas Gallaudet and the schools he created, as well as about the history of American Sign Language. As a part of his final presentation, he invited his sister's teacher and two high school students who were hearing-impaired to join him, and he conducted a live interview in front of our class. Fifth graders asked great questions (Can you talk on the phone with friends? How do you know if the doorbell rings?) and cheered as the high schoolers showed how they were practicing verbal speech.

Students can engage in meaningful research at any age. This isn't just a strategy for upper elementary, middle school, and high school learners. In a preschool class, students became interested in animals' homes. Their teacher explained to me that the adults in the room observe children's play carefully and try to notice interests and themes as they arise. Students were building animals' homes with blocks and pretending to be animals in the dramatic play area. So the teachers in the room worked with this theme. They found books to read aloud that involved animals' homes and took nature walks, looking for holes in the ground and bird and squirrel nests in trees. Students collected bugs and insects and made homes for them in terrariums in the classroom and spent lots of time observing and asking questions. Teachers helped extend children's play in the classroom and introduced new vocabulary words such as habitat, den, and burrow.

FAQ: What about kids who aren't interested in anything?

Remember the scene from *Ferris Bueller's Day Off* where Cameron and Sloane are walking, talking, and holding hands (while Ferris lip-syncs "Danke Schoen" on the parade float in the background)? They're looking ahead to the future.

Cameron: I don't know what I'm going to do.
Sloane: College.
Cameron: Yeah. But to do what?
Sloane: What are you interested in?
Cameron: Nothing.
Sloane: Me neither.

If you work with older children—ones whose curiosity seems to have been a casualty of overly scripted and structured learning in school—you can help rekindle their spark. Get to know your students to find out what they like to do outside of school. Have the class generate lists of questions they have as you explore content. Help students develop new interests and passions through exposing them to new ideas and content in interesting and intriguing ways.

How Extrinsic Motivational Systems Can Diminish Students' Sense of Curiosity

One of the most devastating impacts of extrinsic motivation systems is that they direct children's attention away from what they're interested in and curious about. If you want to get an *A*, you need to pay attention to what the teacher or the textbook thinks is important. If you want to get a Star of the Week award and have your name highlighted on the bulletin board, compliance is likely the way to get there. It's awfully hard to be curious if you're constantly worried about being right.

Intrinsic Motivators Are Interconnected

It's important to recognize the many interconnections of the six intrinsic motivators. Though some might be more prominent in certain activities, they often blend together and get all tangled up. Or one might lead to another. As a child plays a math game, the rolling of the dice and moving a piece around a game board might be fun. However, playing with a friendly peer and engaging in an appropriately challenging task feeds students' needs for belonging and competence. Curiosity might lead a child into a research project about Venus, but if the research project itself is too easy or too hard, curiosity may fade as frustration builds. In an incredible documentary about a man who dives every day in a kelp forest on the coast of South Africa, Craig Foster develops a special bond with an octopus and follows her life for an entire year (Foster, Ehrlich, & Reed, 2020). This drove him to learn everything he could about octopi and the surrounding sea life and eventually led to a sense of purpose—to both document his journey and begin an organization dedicated to preserving natural habitats. Here we see curiosity, purpose, and belonging all in action at once.

We should also recognize that different people are sparked by different intrinsic motivators in different situations. During a math game, some students might feel more energized by the challenge than the belonging, while for others, belonging is more important than fun. So in Chapters 6–8, as we explore how to integrate intrinsic motivators into all that we do, let's not be hypercritical or overly sensitive about which intrinsic motivator is in action at any given time. When we design learning environments and activities that draw on many intrinsic motivators, the chances that students will be inspired and excited increase, and that's what's most important!

Conclusion

Here is our great challenge. If we're going to ditch sticker charts, star rewards programs, clip charts, gem jars, and other incentive systems, and if we're going to stop using traditional grades and the promise and threat of rewards and punishments to motivate students' learning and behavior, then we will have to make sure the work itself is worth doing—from the perspective of the students. We'll need to make sure that the work is so compelling that, if the door were to open, students would choose to stay. Instead of viewing school as a place where teachers make students do work, we need to envision schools where teachers help students uncover their passions, pursue their interests, and become more skilled learners.

Without elements of autonomy, purpose, competence, belonging, curiosity, or fun, it will be almost impossible for schoolwork to feel like anything more than exercises in compliance. These six intrinsic motivators are critical, but they're not enough. Anyone who has ever designed an incredible learning experience infused with these qualities knows this. After an initial burst of enthusiasm, students' motivation wanes as a project moves forward. Or students who are energized and excited about learning get overwhelmed or frustrated, and they give up midstream.

In the next chapter, we'll explore the second key ingredient to supporting self-motivation in our students. We'll look at how to help students learn the skills of self-management they need to follow through on their interests and goals. We'll explore a few critical teacher mindsets and capacities that we must adopt for these motivators to truly work. We'll also explore how to teach students skills and strategies of self-motivation and self-management so they have the ability to follow through on their intrinsic motivations.

5

Teaching Self-Motivation and Self-Management

Don Murray won the Pulitzer Prize for editorial writing in 1954. He authored more than a dozen books about writing and the teaching of writing. He was an adored English professor at the University of New Hampshire and a longtime columnist for the *Boston Globe*. I was sitting in his living room one fall afternoon in the last year of his life, talking about writing (of course). Don was still an imposing figure in his 80s—tall and robust, with sparkling eyes and a full white beard. I was struggling with a book I was working on, and he was offering some advice about getting unstuck. He didn't have idealistic dreamy visions of inspirational writing—quite the contrary. He viewed writing as a blue-collar job, where you grabbed your lunch pail and hard hat before heading to the computer. Don didn't believe in writer's block. "Mike! Does a carpenter get carpenter's block? No! Does an electrician get electrician's block? No! They get to a problem and figure it out!" He then leaned in, looked straight in my eyes, and pointed his finger at me for emphasis. "Do you know what the most important muscle is in a writer's body? The gluteus maximus—'cause you have to sit your butt down and *write!*"

Motivation doesn't do anyone much good without the skills and strategies of self-management. You might be inspired and motivated to run a marathon, but if you can't force yourself to lace up your sneakers and get outside, all the motivation in the world isn't going to get you across the finish line. Also, motivation isn't something that you either have or you don't. It comes and goes. Some days you can be fired up and energized about work, and other days it might feel more like a slog. To keep moving forward with work when the going gets tough, we need strategies to manage ourselves and even manage our motivation.

These are critical skills to teach to our students. Even if work is chock-full of intrinsic motivators and students are initially excited and ready to go, we should expect that there will be bumps along the road. We need to help students learn skills of self-management and self-motivation so they can be successful with the work they care about.

This won't just serve students well in the moment when they're with us in school. Self-motivation and self-management are critically important skills students will need as they move on from school to the workplace. As more and more people telecommute, start their own businesses, and work for themselves in the gig economy, the ability to keep yourself going with work is important. Even people who are still working in more traditional jobs, in more traditional workplace sites, need skills of self-management and self-motivation. Remember that question I asked of parents at a talk in Los Angeles—the ones who helped hire people for their organizations? Companies and organizations are looking for people who are self-motivated and can self-manage.

That's what we'll tackle in this chapter. How can we help students learn skills of self-management? What are some strategies of self-management and self-motivation that, when coupled with work that is intrinsically motivating, can help students turn desire into action? And how do we teach these skills?

Important Teacher Characteristics for Teaching Self-Motivation and Self-Management

Teaching skills and strategies of self-motivation and self-management is a lot harder than the traditional carrot-and-stick approach. It's easier to offer kids incentives for doing what you want than it is to help them learn strategies for managing themselves. The following teacher characteristics can help, so we must nurture these in ourselves. If we don't, we may get frustrated and revert back to traditional patterns.

Patience: The Ability to Delay Gratification

Extrinsic motivators are fantastic for short-term motivation and quick results. If you want your class to be really motivated for the next 20 minutes, offer them an incentive. We now know, however, that this will only work if kids know how to focus, and the messages this incentive sends will do damage to students' long-term motivation and drive. They'll be a little less interested in academic work tomorrow.

This means that we'll need to keep our eye on long-term gains, even in the face of short-term challenges. When a student or a group of students has low energy and they're not feeling motivated about their work, we need to resist the urge to swoop in and deliver the instant jolt of energy. Instead, we might need to adjust the lesson or activity, offer students some other ideas about self-management or motivation strategies they might try, or just breathe a bit and remember that some days are harder than others.

Flexible Thinking: One Size Does Not Fit All

One of the most devastating impacts of the standards movement over the past few decades has been the erosion of teacher creativity and flexibility. And this is by no means a knock on teachers. Scripted programs have stripped teachers of voice and autonomy as they have attempted to deliver a canned and prescribed program to the "average" student. This has been a highly flawed approach, a phenomenon described brilliantly by Todd Rose in his book *The End of Average* (2016). He points out that because people are unique and all have various strengths and challenges (one student might be a strong analytical thinker but struggle with creativity, while another might be a highly skilled oral communicator but struggle with writing), a curriculum designed for an average student fits no one well. He illustrates this with a story about how the U.S. Air Force solved the problem of its high accident rate in the 1940s. Pilots were all flying in planes with cockpits designed for the average pilot. The seats were designed for someone of the average height, controls were situated to be within reach for the average arm length, and so on. A scientist tasked with figuring out why so many planes were crashing crunched some data—the physical dimensions of 4,063 Air Force pilots—and he discovered something astounding. Not a single pilot was average in all 10 of the most important physical traits. There was no average pilot, so they were all flying in cockpits that didn't fit any of them. The solution was now rather obvious: adjustable cockpits. You benefit from the same technology every time you get into a car someone else has driven and need to move the seat forward or backward, adjust the rearview and sideview mirrors, and adjust the position of the steering wheel.

As teachers, we need to design learning for highly variable students who all come to us with various strengths, interests, and needs. This is the main idea behind Universal Design for Learning, a framework for teaching and learning developed by the Center for Applied Special Technology. We need to design learning with adjustable seats and mirrors. This is much different, by the way, than designing 25 different cockpits in your classroom. Instead, we need to design flexible learning experiences that can be adjusted *by the students.* And (and this is a big *and*) we need to teach students how to adjust their learning. (We'll explore a few key ideas behind facilitating student choice well in Chapter 6.)

One way to plan for variability is to work at integrating several different intrinsic motivators into lessons and activities. After all, we aren't all motivated equally by each of the intrinsic motivators, and what motivates us can change given the situation. For example, as a runner, I am most motivated by a sense of competence and fun. Though I enjoy running with others (belonging) and love training for races (purpose), I can continue to be motivated to run even if I'm alone or there aren't races on the horizon. Instead, I fuel my sense of competence by logging how many miles I run each week and challenging myself with speed and endurance workouts. For fun, I love to find new places to run and always make sure I've got different music playlists loaded onto my exercise watch. My wife Heather, on the other hand, runs for different reasons—the health benefits (purpose) and staying connected with her running buddy, Carla (belonging).

This will be true of your students as well. By offering a few options for learning that each connect with different motivators, you'll more likely help kids connect with ones that matter to them. For example, if middle school students can choose a book to read that connects with a specific theme (such as the hero's journey), some might feel empowered by having choice (autonomy), while others might care more about finding a book that connects with their interests (curiosity) or one that is at a just-right challenge level (competence). When it's time to share what they've learned with others, the connection with other students (belonging) might matter more to some students, while the sense of purpose gained by sharing might be more important to others.

Later in this chapter, you'll explore various strategies to share with students to support their self-motivation and self-management. Keep this same idea in mind. Some strategies will work for some students, and different ones will be best for others. You can still teach the strategies to all students, and then guide them as they find the ones that will be the best fit.

Self-Reflection: Cultivating Your Own Self-Motivation

Imagine trying to teach someone to knit if you don't knit yourself. Imagine trying to coach football if you have never played football. Can you teach someone to dance if you don't dance?

Part of helping others learn about self-motivation and self-management is to engage in deep self-reflection about your own motivation and management strategies. I've certainly been conscious of this myself as I've been working on this book. Several have really helped me along the way: Giving myself permission to write a crummy first draft, tracking my progress, taking things one bite at a time, and being realistic about my own motivation have been several of the most helpful. As you explore the strategies that follow, make sure to think about which ones are most helpful for you. Also think of other strategies you use and consider which ones might work for your students. Try some out yourself to strengthen your own skills of self-motivation and self-management. By all means, don't limit yourself to the ideas shared in this chapter—this list is meant as a jumping-off point, not as a definitive and exhaustive list.

Finally, make sure to share your own stories of motivation (and your struggles with motivation) with your students. Consider yourself a master learner who is imparting your skills and strategies to apprentices. And this brings us to perhaps the most important mindset of all.

A Mindset of Teacher as Lead Learner

In the factory model of education, teachers are seen as bosses—overseers who dole out tasks and then ensure that these tasks are completed. It's the teacher's job to get kids to do stuff that they probably don't want to do. Or to look at this in a more positive light, it's the teacher's job to inspire and motivate. Remember, though—if the teacher is doing the motivating, the energy is coming from the wrong place.

We don't just want to energize students in the moment (this class, this unit, this semester, this year), we want to help them on their journey toward being lifelong learners who have the mindsets, skills, and strategies to accomplish their goals and reach for their dreams. This requires a shift in our role. It's now our job to set the conditions, create the environments, and help design learning tasks where students' learning can flourish. We need to make sure that classrooms are safe and supportive environments. We must build positive and supportive relationships with our students so we can guide and coach them well.

There's an important shift we may need to make as we consider the role of teaching content as well. When I made this shift myself, it helped change everything.

My first year of teaching, I was excited to teach science. I had taken a great college class all about hands-on science teaching, and I was eager to bring excitement and enthusism for science to my students. One of the units we worked on that first year was about weather and air pressure, and for some reason, I decided that Bernoulli's principle was something everyone needed to learn. (In case you're rusty on Bernoulli's principle, it's about how fast-moving fluids create areas of low pressure. It's why the tarp on a truck billows out when a truck is driving on the highway, and it's why the shower curtain moves in toward the running water when you turn the shower on.) We did all kinds of cool demonstrations. We held two pieces of paper up and blew between them to watch them move together. We made paper airplanes. We stuck straws in cups and blew across the top of the straw with another, spraying each other with water. When I asked, "What's Bernoulli's principle?" 4th graders would chant, "High-speed winds create an area of low pressure!" I made this the password required for leaving and entering the room. I told all of them: "When you come back and visit me next year, I'm going to ask you about Bernoulli's principle, and you'd better remember!"

The next August, I was setting up my classroom, and sure enough, some of these students who I had the year before popped by for visits. "Hey! How are you all doing?" I asked eagerly. "What's Bernoulli's principle?" Guess how many students remembered? One—Justin, a student who later would go on to win an episode of *Jeopardy!* (I think he already knew Bernoulli's principle before I taught the science unit.)

Was I a failure as a teacher? If the goal was memory—for students to recall Bernoulli's principle six months after they learned about it—then, yes, I suppose I was. However, if the goal was excitement and interest in science, then that unit was a huge success. Parents had told me about how their kids were coming home and performing the science demonstrations for their families. Kids would cheer when science rolled around during the day.

If our ultimate goal is to help build empowered, enthusiastic, and self-motivated learners, then we can start viewing the content we teach as the raw material with which we work. Calculus can be about helping students engage in abstract thinking and solving multistep problems. Learning about various forms of poetry can be about being playful with words, appreciating beauty, and trying different kinds of writing. Any content can be a vehicle for helping students develop interests, follow through on goals, and learn skills and strategies of self-motivation and self-management.

When to Teach These Strategies

Before we get to *what* strategies to teach and *how* to teach them, let's first consider *when* to teach them. The most important idea here is to teach the skills when they are immediately usable to students. We can't teach a strategy in September and then expect kids to use it in November. The skills require context and an immediate chance to try them out and practice them to be most effective.

There are three specific times during work that self-motivation and self-management can be hard, and these are especially good times to teach strategies for kids to try.

1. **Getting started:** It can be hard to get going on a project or assignment, even when you really want to do it. Students might feel overwhelmed, nervous about being successful, or just not sure of how to start.

2. **In the middle:** In the midst of work, especially work that takes a good bit of time, it can be challenging to maintain focus and positive energy. Students might sometimes want to give up when they get frustrated, or they might not know how to recover from a setback.

3. **Crossing the finish line:** As a piece of work comes to a close, it can be challenging to keep the energy high and to finish it off. Students who struggle with perfectionism might want to keep adding one more thing. Some might struggle with aspects of work (editing, final details) that aren't as engaging as the work in the middle.

As students are working, consider what aspects of the work might be challenging at any given time, and then offer strategies both proactively and reactively as needed.

Strategies to Teach

The following strategies are meant to be a starting point. They come from my experience as a classroom teacher and years of working with teachers as a staff developer. I have also drawn from my own experiences as a writer, developer, and independent consultant. As someone who is self-employed, I've had to find lots of self-management strategies to keep my work on track! As you review these strategies, think about which ones might be especially helpful for the students you teach, and consider how you might adapt them to suit the ages, grades, and settings in which you teach.

Take One Bite at a Time

You've probably heard this punchline in response to the joke "How do you eat an elephant?" Sometimes it's hard to start a piece of work or it's hard to keep moving forward if the task feels overwhelming—like eating an elephant. Offer students some ideas about how to break a large task down into smaller ones. For example, they might make a checklist of the smaller tasks within a larger one and check them off as they go.

Set Goals Around Time, Not Task Completion

Sometimes it's hard to get started because tasks feel overwhelming. To take this stress off the table, encourage students to plan short work sessions (10–30 minutes, depending on the age and stamina of the student) followed by short breaks. So instead of thinking, "I have to sit down and write a five-page essay (or complete 25 math problems, etc.)," they might say, "I'm going to work on this essay for 20 minutes and then take a short break."

Tackle an Easy Task First

It might be helpful to start a larger body of work by taking on some easier tasks first. For example, in a set of math problems, use a few simple problems to warm up. Or when working on a research presentation, it might feel easier to work on a visual aid before trying to work on the presentation itself. Sometimes a little momentum makes all the difference!

Tackle a Hard Task First

On the other hand, it might make sense to start with a hard part of the work—when your energy is fresh and creativity is high. For example, when working on a longer piece of writing, students might draft a new section of a paper when they first sit down to work, and then, when their energy starts to wane, they can take on a more mundane, less challenging task such as looking up new resources to explore the next day.

Track Your Progress

When you're feeling a bit overwhelmed, it can help to look at different parts of a project and create guesstimates of how much progress you have made (e.g., "I've completed about 75 percent of step 1, about 50 percent of step 2, and 25 percent of step 3"). Then, as you keep working, update the progress percentages. Sometimes being able to even bump 75 percent to 80 percent after 15 minutes of work helps boost your sense of accomplishment—giving a jolt of energy to keep working. (This strategy was really helpful as I worked on this book!)

Leave Something Unfinished to Return to Later

It can sometimes be hard to reengage with a piece of work after you've taken a break. If students are struggling with this, offer the idea of leaving something unfinished so they have a good starting place when they come back to it. Even leaving a sentence unfinished in a piece of writing can be enough. When the writer sits back down to continue writing, having a sentence to finish can get them back into the flow of their work.

Take Breaks

Short movement breaks, even a quick walk to get some water or a stand-and-stretch break, can reenergize learning by sending oxygen to the brain. As a class, you might generate some lists of things to do when taking a break either at school or home (listen to one song, walk around the block, get a drink of water or a quick snack) and some strategies for keeping breaks short (set a timer, don't check your phone, etc.).

Do Yoga Poses

You might teach a few simple yoga poses to your students—ones they can use as a brief brain break or reset after they've been distracted or gotten off track. It's amazing how reenergized one feels after some deep breathing and a few rounds of the sun salutation or the tree pose!

Consider Body Position When Working

Our minds are connected with our bodies, and the body postures we hold affect how we learn. Have students consider body positions that best match the kind of work they're doing. Lying on the floor or your bed might be fine for listening to a podcast or watching a TED talk, but it would probably be uncomfortable to type that way for long. Sitting or standing at a desk or table is probably a better idea.

Turn Off Your Inner Censor

You know that little voice in the back of your ear, whispering to you as you work—discouraging things such as "This isn't good enough," "You just misspelled a word," and "Couldn't you be doing a better job right now?" Sometimes when you're typing and you see the little red squiggly line appear under a word, you feel compelled to go back and fix it in the moment. Or when you write something and glance back and realize you could have worded something a bit more cleanly, you erase a sentence and try again. These kinds of small breaks in concentration can kill your momentum when working on a draft of something, where spelling and initial wording don't matter. Try covering your screen with a piece of paper as you work. Focus on what you're doing, not on how it looks. Then you can go back and clean things up later on. Remember the old adage: *Perfect is the enemy of good.*

Be Open to Feedback

We can learn so much from other people's feedback, but it can also be hard to stay open to that feedback. It requires a bit of emotional vulnerability. Students have to be willing to let go of their ego and really listen to others. In addition to modeling and eliciting ideas from students (strategies we'll get to in a bit), you might consider using structures that encourage students to be open to feedback. For example, when students are conferring, and it's the job of one student to offer advice, make the rule that the student who is receiving feedback isn't allowed to respond. They can jot notes and then decide later whether to incorporate the advice they've been given. This simple rule—that you can't talk when receiving advice—can build in a bit of safety for both the giver and receiver. The giver doesn't have to worry about the receiver's reaction, and the receiver doesn't have to agree with the giver's point of view. Additionally, if the receiver can't push back on the advice in the moment, it gives them some more time to think about whether or not to incorporate their peer's idea.

Screen Out Distractions

It's easy to say to students, "Find a good place to work—someplace without distractions." And sure, it would be great if everyone could do that, but this just isn't a reality for many people—either in the classroom or at home. So we might also offer students suggestions for how to minimize distractions. For example, if you're working in a room with a lot of movement, try turning to face a wall so you see less of the action. If a space has lots of noise—people talking, a TV blaring, dishes clinking—try using headphones with white noise playing. (YouTube has tons of videos that can be used for background noise: waves on a beach, a train rolling on the tracks, distant city noises, etc.)

You might also help students identify temptations that can get in the way of work. For example, if they're going to be tempted to pick up their phone every time it buzzes, they might set it on airplane mode during work intervals and then check messages during breaks. Or for younger children, if there are toys nearby that could be tempting, encourage them to put them out of sight during work times.

FAQ: What about playing music while you work?

Kids will often make the case that music helps them focus. Sometimes it can. Soothing, quiet music played in the background can be a way to screen out distractions or put one in a mood for working. Encourage students who are asking to play music while they work to reflect on whether it's really helping or not. Does the music help clear their mind, or are they actually thinking about the music instead of work? Can they turn music on and leave it alone, or does the music require constant management (adjusting the volume, searching for the next good song, etc.)? For students who want to play music as they work, you might suggest some artists or genres that you think might support focused attention.

Use Self-Talk

When I ask teachers about which self-management strategies they use the most, some variation of self-talk is the most commonly expressed strategy. Teachers say things like, "I say to myself, 'You're almost there. You can do it' or 'You only have a little bit more to go.'" This is a strategy we can teach our students, helping them be more mindful—and intentional—about the messages they feed themselves.

Utilize Productive Times of Day

This strategy works best when students have flexible time to work, such as when structuring at-home learning time or considering how to use open-ended work periods in school. Have students identify the times of day when they have the best energy for work. Then encourage them to tackle tasks that involve deep concentration or creativity during those times. My son, for example, often gets a crazy burst of creative and productive energy late in the evening—it's a great time for him to get work done. I, on the other hand, do my best work in the morning. Save simpler tasks, ones that don't require great energy, for other times of the day.

Procrastinate Productively

We probably all procrastinate about something at some point. And while we certainly want to avoid procrastinating, when it happens, at least we can make it productive time. My daughter loves this strategy. She was recently putting off a challenging piece of schoolwork, so she took care of lots of other smaller and easier work items while procrastinating on the tough one. When the deadline for the one she was avoiding neared, she panicked a bit and got it done. She was exhausted, but she said, "I did so much productive procrastination that now I have almost all of my work for the rest of the week finished!"

Recognize the Blessing of a Deadline

This is another of Don Murray's favorite sayings: "There's nothing like the blessing of a deadline." It's easy to procrastinate when there aren't deadlines or when they're far away, so one thing students could do is create their own mini deadlines as they break a big project up into smaller chunks. They could then trade deadlines with a peer so they can help each other be responsible for meeting their goals.

Build Stamina Over Time

Someone just getting into running doesn't start by lacing up and running a marathon. Instead, they start with short and gentle runs and then build up over time. We can help children consider how to build their work stamina over time. Perhaps they can start with 5–10 minutes of independent work time early on before needing a break. Then, later in the year, they can set goals for longer work times—eventually building to 30–45 minutes or longer (depending on their age and temperament).

Know When to Stop Working

It can be a huge mistake to try and push through and keep working when you're exhausted or overly frustrated. Not only are you likely to crash and burn emotionally, but you're probably doing poor work, which will require time and energy later on to clean up. Teach students to know when it's time to stop working and get away for a bit.

FAQ: What about rewarding yourself? Does that damage motivation in the long run?

We now know how much damage to motivation extrinsic rewards can do, but what if a student wants to set up their own incentive system? Is this a good self-management strategy? For example, what if a student wants to reward themselves with 15 minutes of video game time after doing 45 minutes of work on a school project? Would the same damage be done to motivation?

We should approach this with caution. To use an if-then reward system on ourselves ("If I work for 45 minutes, then I get to play video games for 15 minutes") might still lead to crowding out and satiation—especially if it becomes the go-to strategy. Eventually, a larger and larger reward might be needed to garner enough motivation to accomplish the task, and the same negative message is being sent about the work itself (i.e., the work is so boring I need to bribe myself with video games to get it done), which could decrease long-term interest in learning.

On the other hand, one of the key takeaways from self-determination theory is that autonomy is probably the most important of the intrinsic motivators (Ryan & Deci, 2000). So if students create their own incentive system, their autonomy is not being diminished as it would be if someone else imposed an if-then reward system on them. In fact, they might be boosting their sense of autonomy through this exercise.

My suggestion is that this kind of self-imposed if-then incentive system be used sparingly. There are so many other strategies to use. However, perhaps with a big deadline approaching just as the weather is warming up in the spring, dangling the carrot of playing outside after a certain amount of time or after completing a specific part of the work might be just what students need to get themselves across the finish line.

What Are Other Strategies You Use?

The list offered in this section is hardly exhaustive. What are other strategies of self-management and self-motivation that you know of or that you use when you're working? Make sure to draw from your own experience as well as that of friends and colleagues. Ask people you know who seem to be highly productive what strategies they use to get so much done.

How to Teach Them

Now that you have a bunch of strategies you might teach, it's time to consider a few ways to teach them. Again, let's remember that these strategies need to be taught in the moment—right when students have the chance to apply them. One of the biggest mistakes I see schools and districts making is that they view the teaching of social and emotional skills as a separate curriculum—something you do during an SEL block on Tuesday and Thursday afternoons or only during advisory periods or morning meetings. Instead, we can use the following strategies as part of our academic teaching, weaving them right into the fabric of lessons, activities, and units.

Another common mistake we sometimes make is that we confuse telling kids about strategies with actually teaching the strategies. Now, certainly, there are times we might simply share a strategy or a piece of advice with students, but strategies are more likely to stick with students if their learning is active and interactive. The following three strategies can be used with just about any age and grade.

Effective Modeling

I was working with a group of 2nd graders just a few days before a holiday break, and to say that they had some energy is a vast understatement. We were playing a math game, and they could hold it together for a minute or two before they'd spring into the air like grasshoppers. I decided to model a simple self-regulation strategy that they could try. "I know you're all so excited. This game is really fun! It's hard to play it, though, when your body is bouncing up and down. I'm going to show you a strategy that you could try for keeping your energy under control." I then modeled the strategy— showing how to pinch two fingers together, giving a little pressure. "What do you see me doing?" I asked. One girl raised her hand and ventured, "You're pushing your fingers together. Are you pushing hard?" I replied, "Not really, just hard enough to feel some pressure. It helps me stay focused when I'm feeling bouncy." Most of the kids were already trying it, but I encouraged everyone, "Try it out and see how it feels. Notice how you can focus on pushing your fingers together, and that can help the rest of your body stay calm." Students all pushed their fingers together, and their bodies, were indeed noticeably more still. "As we keep playing the math game, if you feel yourself starting to get bouncy, you might try that strategy," I offered. About five minutes later, I noticed that one of the students—Anthony—had his hand down next to his hip, and he was squeezing his fingers together. I leaned in and whispered, "Are you trying the strategy?" and he whispered back, "Yep."

Modeling is such a powerful strategy. There are four key components to use when modeling with students:

1. **State the goal.** Let students know what you're about to model and why. Be as crisp and direct with this goal as possible.
2. **Demonstrate.** Give students a positive demonstration of the skill or strategy. (Model what *to do*, not what *not* to do.)
3. **Reflect.** Students need a chance to reflect on what they've seen. They might have a partner chat, do some quiet thinking, jot a few notes, or participate in a brief class discussion.
4. **Practice.** Students should have a chance to practice the skill or strategy right away.

These four components can then be mixed and matched depending on the complexity of what you're modeling and the age and experience of the students. Though you should probably almost always start by stating the goal and demonstrating, after that, you might have students reflect, demonstrate again, reflect again, give everyone a chance to practice, and then reflect one more time. The key is to give students enough scaffolding and support so they can be successful, without overdoing things and dragging out the modeling too long. Also, keep in mind that one modeling session probably won't be enough. You may need to return and remodel some skills and strategies many times.

Eliciting Ideas from Students

Sometimes students don't need explicit modeling. If a skill or strategy is more familiar or if it's more open-ended, you might instead ask students for some of their ideas about how to be successful with a strategy or skill. Check out the example below to see how this might sound.

> **Teacher:** It can be really hard to work in a space where there's a lot of activity. Today we're going to generate some ideas together. First, let's think about this in pairs before we share ideas with the whole group. You have one minute to chat with your partner. What are some ways someone might screen out distractions in a space where there's a lot going on?
> The students chat together for one minute.

Teacher: OK. Let's think of some ideas together. I'll chart the ideas so we don't lose track of any. Who'd like to start? Jamilla, do you have one?

Jamilla: Jamie and I talked about trying to find a quiet space—away from the activity. Like, if I'm trying to work in my apartment, if everyone's in the kitchen, I go to the couch in the next room over.

The teacher records *find a quiet space*.

Teacher: OK, there's one idea. Who has another? Mark—your hand is up.

Mark: You could turn your back to people.

Teacher: Could you say a bit more about that? What do you mean?

Mark: I mean, if you turn away from people who are making a lot of noise, maybe you won't be as distracted 'cause you can't see them so easy.

The teacher writes *turn away from people*.

Teacher: Hani, you have an idea to add?

Hani: Yeah. Me and my partner talked about putting in earbuds and listening to quiet music. Sometimes that helps block out stuff.

Teacher: How do you keep the music itself from being a distraction?

Hani: You have to put on something relaxing, and then not fool around with it.

The teacher writes *relaxing music*.

Teacher: We'll add some more ideas to this list later. For now, turn and talk with your partner again. Which of these three ideas do you think might help you? Share a bit about why.

The students chat together for one minute.

Teacher: As you're working and there's some commotion, you might try one of these ideas out. We'll check in again tomorrow to see if any of these were helpful. Also, keep track of other strategies you try so we can add those to our list.

There are a few things you might have noticed about this session. First off, it was short. Even with the two one-minute partner chats, this whole session took about five minutes. You also might have noticed that the students talked about as much as the teacher (much more if you count the partner chats). That's important. The ideas should be coming from the students.

Also, you might have noticed that at the end, the teacher invited students to try a strategy. It can be tempting to use stronger language such as "You all need to pick one and try it," but I've found this can be counterproductive. It shifts the energy away from the students and back to the teacher, and how would you hold students accountable for something like this anyway? The more we can keep the ownership with the students, the more authentic it will be.

Fishbowl

Sometimes it can be helpful for students to watch others try a strategy. In the fishbowl strategy, several students try out an activity or practice a skill while others stand around them observing and taking notes. (The students practicing are like fish, and the observers are looking into the fishbowl.) Afterwards, the students who observed share some of what they observed and noticed.

This can be an incredibly powerful strategy when used well. Students on the inside of the fishbowl have an opportunity to assume the role of model and demonstrate important skills. Observers have the important job of noticing what they see and being ready to share and reflect. If you're going to try this strategy, here are a few suggestions to help it stay safe and supportive:

- **Only take volunteers to be inside the fishbowl.** Even if you know a student would do really well as a model, don't force anyone to be observed who isn't up for it. The potential downside of having a student feel embarrassed in front of others isn't worth the risk.
- **Set students up for success.** Make sure students inside the fishbowl know what their role is and what they should be modeling. You might even practice a bit ahead of time. Make sure students on the outside know exactly what they should be looking for so that their observations are targeted and on task.
- **Have students model only appropriate behaviors.** Just like with regular modeling, only have students demonstrate what *to do,* not what *not* to do. This will help everyone be clear about the positive attributes of whatever they're exploring.

Conclusion

I worry that sometimes we send unrealistic messages to kids about motivation and work. "You should always try your best!" and "We should always give 100 percent!" are easy to say (and might look catchy on a T-shirt or in a sports drink commercial), but is that really what we expect? I think sometimes it's fine to just make it through a work period without the expectation of "trying your best."

The reality is that sometimes work is a slog, even when it's something you care deeply about. Being self-motivated isn't about always having high energy and wanting to do work. It's often more about being able to keep yourself going when the going gets tough. It's when we're doing meaningful work—something that fills us with purpose, that we have some control over, that we're curious about, and so on—that we can truly practice skills of perseverance and grit. When intrinsic motivators are present and students have skills of self-management, they can really practice self-motivation.

So now it's time to think more specifically about what this looks like in various aspects of the school day. How do we infuse academics and classroom management with intrinsic motivation? How do we create cultures of self-motivation in our classrooms and schools?

6

Curricula and Instructional Strategies

Let's return to the story about my students who created their own version of a documentary about the Lewis and Clark adventure. Why was this project so compelling? Remember—this was a really challenging group with diverse and complex social, emotional, and academic needs. They had a hard time focusing on work and were easily bored and distracted. It was a successful math lesson if we could make it 10 minutes before they started to fall apart. In Chapter 4, this story illustrated belonging as a motivator. Now let's consider this project through the lens of all six intrinsic motivators.

- **Autonomy.** This was a student-driven project. The idea for making a movie came from them, and they had a lot of voice and choice about roles to play in the production.
- **Belonging.** This was a team effort. Everyone had a role to play and contributed to the success of the project. They encouraged and supported each other along the way.
- **Competence.** Students became incredibly knowledgeable about this story—gaining a sense of mastery about the event. This was also really hard—which gave a sense of challenge during the work and a sense of accomplishment at the end.
- **Curiosity.** Students took on roles that leveraged their interests. Some did more writing, while others took lead roles with the artwork. Their

fascination with the story of Lewis and Clark—which they discovered while watching the film—drove their enthusiasm as they recreated it. (After all, what 5th grader isn't going to want to be a part of reen-acting Sergeant Floyd's death scene or be moved—pun intended—by the idea of Dr. Benjamin Rush's powerful laxatives known as "Rush's Thunderbolts"?)

- **Fun.** Creating costumes and coloring the scenery for backgrounds was enjoyable. Practicing lines was hard but satisfying. Countless scenes had to be shot over and over again as kids collapsed into giggles, which, of course, led to the inevitable blooper reel.
- **Purpose.** This may have been the most powerful motivator of them all. We were creating a movie to show to real audiences. Kids fretted about quality. They struggled with which scenes to include and which ones to cut. They cared. This was real work.

I also worked to support and extend students' skills of self-management throughout this project. There were many times where some kids had breaks in the action. For example, once we were filming, sometimes only seven or eight students would be directly involved. Other students had a variety of independent work to choose from during these times: independent reading, working on writing pieces for writing workshop, catch-up or extensions of math work for the unit we were working on, and so on. We brainstormed ways for students to stay focused on independent work even while others were acting and the camera was rolling. (The most common strategy was to move away from the action—moving to a quiet spot in the room or sitting in the hallway to get some work done.) I also shared many strategies for emo-tional regulation and conflict resolution as a part of this process. There were times when kids would collapse into giggling fits while filming (which is fine, up to a point), and there were other times when tempers flared as kids disagreed about how a scene should play out, what the background should look like, or any one of a myriad of other minor issues. (This class didn't shy away from conflict.)

In Chapter 4, we explored a few examples of what it looks like when autonomy, purpose, belonging, competence, curiosity, and fun, are present in schoolwork. In this chapter, we're going to explore this idea in more depth. When your school or district is looking to adopt a new math curriculum or take on a new approach for teaching literacy, what should you look for? What are some key elements of instruction that foster connections to these key six intrinsic motivators?

Students Get Lots of Choice About Academics

Few instructional strategies offer such clear connections to so many of the intrinsic motivators as choice. Even simple choices, such as whether to use markers, crayons, or colored pencils to shade in a graph, offer students a bit of autonomy. Letting students pick one of three novels to read to explore a topic in social studies can help them connect with personal interests (curiosity), cultural relevance (belonging) as they find a character or story they can connect with, or competence as they find a book at an appropriate reading level. Offering students the chance to practice working with fractions, decimals, and percentages by either flipping flash cards, practicing with a partner, or playing a computer game offers up chances to spark autonomy, competence, belonging, and fun.

In addition to (and partially because of) the connections to these motivators, there are many other potential benefits of choice (Anderson, 2016). Here are just a few:

- **Differentiation.** Students can learn to differentiate their own learning to put themselves in their just-right learning zone.
- **Deeper learning.** When the work in the room is more diverse, students get inspired by each other and learn from each other.
- **On-task behavior.** Students engaged in activities of their choice are more likely to stick with them and less likely to become emotionally dysregulated.
- **Social-emotional learning.** Students practice a wide array of social and emotional skills through choice, such as self-awareness, effective decision making, perseverance, social awareness, and more.

There are almost unlimited ways to offer students choices about their daily work. They might get to choose some of what they learn, how they learn it, or how they demonstrate their learning. Students might get simple choices, even within the context of rigid and scripted curricula. For example, on a math page with a bunch of practice problems, students might get to choose the ones that are at the just-right challenge level to solve or make up some of their own. We might also give students more complex choices, such as digging into an independent research project within a theme, or a more open-ended one, such as a Power of One project.

Regardless of the context or complexity of the choice, I suggest working in three phases as you facilitate choice with students. This will help students learn to choose well—finding options that will maximize their own motivation—as well as reflect on their process, building skills of self-reflection, metacognition, and effective decision making, which are all critical self-management skills.

Phase 1: Choose

Before students make their choice and begin to work, give them an opportunity to think carefully about their options and make a choice that aligns with their goals and motivations. Teaching students the self-management skills of how to choose well—finding choices at a good challenge level and ones that align with what they need (even if that's different from what they want) is critical for choice to work well.

Phase 2: Do

Once students have made their choice, they should follow through and engage in the work they chose. Teachers serve as coaches, guiding and supporting students along the way, helping them manage themselves as they work.

Phase 3: Review

After students have finished their work, give them a chance to review their work and reflect on the choice they made. Did their choice work out well? Did they find an option that was fun, appropriately challenging, or interesting? How might they choose differently the next time they have a similar choice? When we help students practice skills of self-reflection and metacognition, they learn from their experience and can become more skilled and independent at making good choices in the future.

FAQ: Should students have freedom and choices about everything?

No! If students are given too much freedom, they may feel overwhelmed by all the possibilities. Additionally, one of the ways we help ignite curiosity is by exposing students to new topics and content. If we always let them choose what to read, for example, they may never break out of their comfort zone and try new genres. We should balance student choice experiences with others where there isn't choice to offer students some autonomy while also helping to broaden their horizons.

Learning Is Cocreated

This is a topic Bena Kallick and Allison Zmuda (2017) address beautifully in *Students at the Center: Personalized Learning with Habits of Mind*. The basic premise of cocreation is to bring students into the conversation about how to structure their learning. What ideas do they have for questions and problems to tackle, how to tackle them, and ways to demonstrate learning? For example, let's say a middle school science class is studying issues of water quality. After a brief introduction to the overall topic and issue, the class might then generate a bunch of questions they'd like to investigate. This could then lead to figuring out how to dig into these questions. Should they start with traditional research in books and online resources? Someone might have a parent who works at a local wastewater processing facility or an aunt who works as a lake biologist at a local university. Perhaps they could join the class as guest speakers. These initial steps then lead to a field trip that fires the class up to share some of what they're learning with the rest of the school. Guided by the teacher and the broad curricular goals, the class creates a learning expedition together. Students' voices and ideas have a significant role in shaping the work.

Here are a few important ideas to consider when students help you shape the work of the classroom.

You Can't Plan Everything Ahead of Time

What's both exciting and a little scary for teachers with work like this is that you don't know what the final product or event will look like before you begin. That can also be liberating, though. When we cocreate learning with students—when we ask them, "What are some things you want to learn, and what are some of your ideas for what we might do?"—we all get to experience the wonder of learning together. Students feel a greater sense of autonomy, as they help shape their learning, as well as belonging, as they do so in community. Their work will also be filled with purpose, as they work toward learning goals they care about. On the other hand, if you enter into a project with students and you have a really clear idea of what the final product and event will look like, it will be hard for this not to feel like an exercise in compliance for students.

Keep Developmental Interests in Mind

There are some predictable topics and themes that children of different ages seem to be interested in. In *Reclaiming Childhood,* William Crain (2003) makes the compelling case that young children are often drawn to and fascinated with the natural world and seem to be predisposed to create imaginative artwork and beautiful poetry. Chip Wood, in his elegant text about applying developmental theory to the classroom, *Yardsticks,* highlights other common typical developmental interests (2007). Children in upper elementary grades are often interested in the study of people and cultures, as well as environmental causes and concerns. As adolescents become more aware of the broader world, they are often interested in current events and yearn to discuss and debate issues. All of these interests can help inform how we help children explore reading, writing, art, music, science, social studies, and nearly any other academic area, and children can help inform the direction the learning takes.

Slow Down and Let Students Observe

Our fast-paced schools too often rush through content, sprinting from one topic to the next. But curiosity can't be rushed. Students need time to think and observe to be curious. Once, as a part of a science unit on local ecosystems, our 5th grade class trudged into the woods behind our school with nets and plastic buckets. We scooped mucky water from a vernal pool, brought it back to the classroom, poured it into an aquarium, and watched as the muck settled and life emerged. This tank remained on a back table for more than a week, and students could sit and observe at various times through the day. They were enthralled. The highlight might have been when someone happened to catch the moment when a dragonfly nymph (which looks like something out of a Godzilla movie) attacked and ate a small tadpole. Someone had the idea of putting an observation notebook next to the tank, and students started to take notes. I placed some field guides next to the tank, and students spontaneously looked up information and tried to identify what they saw. When we give students time and space to be curious, their curiosity can then drive powerful learning that we can support and guide.

Slow Down and Have Students Ask Questions

Why is it that school seems to be all about kids answering questions that someone else has asked? What if we flipped that paradigm, and students were the ones asking the questions? In addition to slowing down to observe, slow down and have kids ask questions. What do they want to know about the American Revolution? What do they wonder about fractions? Especially for older students, this may be difficult. If they've had school experiences that have emphasized answering other people's questions (and even discouraged from asking their own), they may be reluctant to risk asking a "wrong" question. Or their question-asking abilities may have atrophied. We may need to share and teach some specific strategies for how to ask interesting and relevant questions and give students time to practice.

Learning Is Differentiated and Learner Variability Is Assumed

The main idea behind differentiation is to help students work in what Vygotsky called the *zone of proximal development*—the space between what someone can do independently and their potential within that domain (Anderson, 2016). This is all about competence. When learning is too easy, it's boring, and learners shut down. When learning is too hard, it's overly frustrating, and learners shut down. When we can help kids find that space in between what's too easy and too hard, they can experience the joy of stretching themselves and meeting realistic challenges—which is incredibly motivating.

There are other ways learners differ, however, beyond level of challenge, so we should consider how to differentiate in different ways. Some learners might do better work on a task on their own, while others might benefit from working with a partner. One student might best show their understanding of a concept through taking a test, while another might shine in an essay. One student might best learn about an event in the Napoleonic wars by reading articles, while another might be better off with some short videos.

There are many ways to differentiate learning for students. Here are three. The first is an example of differentiated learning. The second two are examples of differentiated instruction.

Choice

As we explored earlier in this chapter, choice is a fantastic vehicle for differentiation. We can teach students how to find just-right books in reading workshop, consider a good way to practice a math skill, or self-select a topic of high interest for an independent study.

Strategy Groups

As we approach the final phase of writing a lab report for a science exploration, we might notice that there are a few different skills students could use help with. So as students are working, we pull one group together to help them with the analysis phase of their work. Another group is struggling with clarity—they're using too many words when describing their process. Yet another group did the experiment, but they didn't really understand what was happening, so that's another group to meet with. Pulling a few small groups to support specific skills enables us to target instruction to those who need it most.

One-on-One Conferences

Conferring with students individually is another way we can offer differentiated instruction. As we sit with each student to support their math work, we may watch how they're tackling a challenge and have them articulate their process. Then we offer a little coaching as they work—tailoring our support to what we know about the students and their learning. As a general rule, conferences are best when they are relatively short (just a few minutes) and only focus on one or two skills at a time.

FAQ: Is strategy grouping the same as ability grouping?

No. Strategy groups are flexible and short-lived, often just for one class period. They provide students with targeted instruction based on skills they're working on in the moment. This can boost their sense of competence as they gain new skills and understandings. Because the groups are ever-changing, students don't develop the self-consciousness and negative self-perceptions that can accompany ability groups. Ability grouping typically involves placing students in tracks or sets that remain relatively stable—"high," "middle," and "low" groups, for example, that might stay together for a quarter, semester, or even a year. Although this might seem to make teaching more convenient for adults, this is a low-impact strategy when it comes to achievement (Hattie, 2009, pp. 89–91). The goal of this strategy may be differentiation, but we can't expect to put students into three inflexible groups and expect each group to all learn in the same way. Learners are too variable for that. Teachers still need to differentiate, even in homogeneous groups.

Work and Learning Are Authentic

One of the ways to ensure a stronger sense of purpose in daily work is to make sure the learning is authentic and real. Students should read real books, not just excerpts and snippets from anthologies. Kids should solve real-world math problems instead of grinding through problem sets on workbook pages. Students should create art pieces for an art show or display—not just to turn in for a grade. Students can explore concepts and ideas in genuine and authentic projects and share them with a real audience.

As you peruse the following examples, notice that many of them can work in many settings: in school, through online learning, and even in a hybrid model. Also consider the skills and strategies you might need to teach students so they can manage themselves and their work effectively.

Whole-Class Projects and Challenges

When a group of students tackles a problem or challenge together, they can build a sense of group membership through academic work. These challenges might be long and complex, such as planning and orchestrating a class trip connected with a unit of study. Or they may be short and simple. For example, the whole class might create a bulletin board display to highlight examples of math problems they're practicing.

Reading Workshop

Incredible literacy learning can happen when students spend lots of time reading and reflecting on books of their choice that are at their just-right reading level. Whole-class lessons, strategy group sessions, and individual conferences provide differentiated learning and specific skill building. Most importantly, kids learn to read while also developing a love of reading.

Writing Workshop

Students have a lot to say. They have stories to tell. In a writing workshop, students practice key writing skills through writing authentic pieces that have personal meaning and significance. As in a reading workshop, teachers facilitate a variety of instructional methods: whole-class lessons, targeted small-group sessions, and individual conferences to teach specific standards and competencies. Students also support each other as writers and learn valuable social and emotional skills as they confer. Writing is also done for a purpose and is shared with an authentic audience. For example, short stories might be read aloud, or persuasive essays or short stories might be compiled in an anthology.

Independent Research Projects

Independent research isn't just for kids like Aaron who have a quirky interest in turtles. All students can learn about something that is interesting, relevant, and meaningful to them, whether they're engaged in a thematic study as a class or investigating more open-ended topics. Students can learn about sports, pets, careers, hobbies, and just about anything else. When they have a chance to share what they've learned with others, students feel a great sense of purpose. I've seen middle and high school students take on topics like climate change, gang violence, systemic racism, and gender inequality. I've seen kindergartners research favorite animals and their habitats.

Community Service Learning

It's incredible how much motivation kids can have when they take on a project to benefit their community. Talk about purpose! Writing letters about reducing the use of disposable plastics, creating spreadsheets to catalogue food items collected for a local food pantry, reading books about animal welfare to help support a local animal shelter—these tasks are real, and they inspire real enthusiasm.

Games

Many boxed curricula offer games, though it seems that they are often offered as if-you-have-time options. Consider playing the games and skipping some of the worksheets. Create worksheet Boggle games with key letter combinations embedded to practice word-study skills. Give students the option of flipping cards or picking up dominos to create their own math problems to solve to make math work more enjoyable. Students can even create their own games and then play them. One year, a 5th grader in my class came up with a version of dodgeball to connect with our study of the American Revolution. In her version, one team was the Patriots and the other the Redcoats (of course!). When a player was knocked out, they went to jail and could be freed later in the game by their teammates. We played it at a Revolutionary War–themed class sleepover, and it was a huge hit!

Open-Ended Exploration

Many schools are experimenting with structures like "genius hour," modeled after Google's 20 percent policy, where developers spend 20 percent of their working time engaged in projects of their own choosing. Many schools are also returning, at long last, to play-based learning, where students have more open-ended time to engage in activities of their choice. I was thrilled when in 2018, New Hampshire amended its law regarding an adequate education (RSA 193-E:2-a, the Substantive Educational Content of an Adequate Education law), requiring a play-based approach in kindergarten:

> Educators shall create a learning environment that facilitates high quality, child-directed experiences based upon early childhood best teaching practices and play-based learning that comprise movement, creative expression, exploration, socialization, and music. Educators shall develop literacy through guided reading and shall provide unstructured time for the discovery of each child's individual talents, abilities, and needs.

Learning Is Culturally Responsive

Does your classroom or school culture reflect the cultures of your students? Do your students see themselves and their cultures reflected in the faculty of your school? Do they see themselves in the content and curricula? This is a hugely important topic, and one that is hard to address briefly, but to exclude it would also be a huge mistake. With that in mind, let's explore one key component of culturally responsive teaching.

Do students see themselves reflected in their school experience? Or do they feel like outsiders who are looking in? If students feel as though their heritage and background aren't reflected in their school, how will they ever feel a significant sense of belonging?

I had the privilege of attending a conference session facilitated by Baruti Kafele, award-winning educator and prolific author and speaker who is, among other things, a champion of supporting and educating Black male students. In a brief exercise, he made this point painfully clear. Striding to the front of the stage, he looked at the audience and pretended to take a picture of us. "I just took your picture. Here it is." He held up a piece of paper and motioned as if he was handing us a photo. "As you look at that picture of this audience, where do you look first?" Several audience members voiced what we were all thinking: "Ourselves." "That's right," Baruti continued. "We always want and need to know how we fit into the picture." He then started to rip pieces out of the paper and held it up for us to see—a Swiss cheese–like photograph. "This is what school looks like for many of our Black and Brown boys. They look around their schools, and they don't see themselves in the picture." So consider your students with this question in mind. Do they see themselves in the books in your classroom library? In the stories you share? In the historical events and people you study? In the scientists and artists you celebrate?

Learning Is Active and Interactive

As you'll see, there are many overlaps between many of these categories. Many of the authentic work and differentiation examples are also active and interactive. Here are some learning strategies that can boost students' sense of fun and belonging. As you explore these ideas, once again consider the skills and strategies you can teach to students so they can be successful with this kind of dynamic learning.

The Arts

Have you ever seen students—perhaps ones old enough that it comes as a bit of a surprise—light up when they're given the chance to color or paint as a part of a science lesson? Singing (and songwriting) can add life and joy to any academic subject. Offer students opportunities to move as they learn. One of my favorite class games is Group Charades. Students are placed in small teams and given a topic within an academic theme. For example, if the category is weather, groups might be assigned topics such as thunderstorm, fog, snow flurry, and cold front. They have a few minutes to plan a short, silent skit (no sound effects, no props) to act out for the class.

Hands-On Learning

Whenever possible, give students the chance to *do* things, not just read about them or watch someone else do them. Working with pattern blocks can help students understand fractions, and base-ten blocks are an incredible tool to help children understand place value and computation. In culinary class, kids should cook just about every day, and science classes should be about kids doing science, not just learning about it. And yes, this all may take a bit more time, but because it's fun and engaging, kids' brains will light up, and they'll actually learn!

Project-Based Learning

When students have the chance to make something, they often feel a great sense of purpose. Creating a story timeline to recap a book or building a tower with blocks to understand volume can be incredibly motivational. Some teachers may worry that projects take too much time, but that's part of why they're so powerful. A student who spends five hours constructing a board game to demonstrate their understanding of Greek myths will think more deeply about content than will a student who spends 10 minutes filling in a worksheet.

Simulations

When each of my kids was in 8th grade, they participated in a simulation of the economics of a colonial town. Students all had different roles—farmers, traders, a tax collector, and others. There were complicated rules to follow and specific goals to achieve, and each class was a flurry of activity as students wheeled-and-dealed, trying to play their own part while also observing the system as a whole.

The World Peace Game (https://worldpeacegame.org/) is another kind of simulation. Again, students have roles and goals, but the game itself is flexible and open-ended, as students try to achieve global prosperity. I've watched this game in action in several schools with both elementary and middle school students, and their focus, intensity, and thoughtfulness are a joy to see.

Skits, Plays, and Movies

Students can create mock weather forecasts, interview each other on talk shows, practice and perform puppet shows, and transform favorite books into movies. These productions can be highly polished endeavors that take weeks or months to produce, or they can be short and informal.

Learning Is Celebrated

Just because we're moving away from incentivizing kids with the promise of ice cream parties and academic awards doesn't mean we can't celebrate students' accomplishments and work. Far from it! Celebrating hard work, learning, and accomplishments is a fantastic way to boost students' sense of competence, and looking forward to the celebrations can add an extra sense of purpose to the work. Not to mention, the celebrations themselves can be fun! The key is to not make the celebration a carrot ("If you do *x*, then we'll have a party"). Here are a few ways to keep school celebrations in line with intrinsic motivation.

They're (Mostly) About Academics

If a school's goal is to ignite passion and curiosity in children as learners, most of the celebrations should be about learning. We can host poetry slams, science fairs, independent research showcases, and math game nights. Whole-school art exhibits and music recitals help children showcase learning in the arts. This doesn't mean we can't hold the occasional pep rally for a sports team or assembly for a fundraising effort, but it does mean that these are the exceptions, not the rule.

They Are Inclusive

All art students should have the chance to show off their learning, not just the "best" artists. All students should get to join an evening celebration with math and literacy games, not just the well-behaved ones who earned the privilege because of their skills of self-regulation.

They're Not Competitive

A school can hold a science fair without offering first, second, and third place ribbons to a few students. We can host a poetry slam without voting for a winner. Emphasize collective accomplishment and celebrate all students' work instead of holding a few students up above the rest.

Teacher Talk Assumes and Reinforces Intrinsic Motivation

The way we talk about learning has a profound impact on how students feel about it. Try using your phone or tablet to create an audio recording of yourself teaching and interacting with students. Use this to analyze your language. Are you using language habits that assume and reinforce students' intrinsic motivation? Use Figure 6.1 as a starting point.

FAQ: What about scripted curricula? It's so common, but it seems to run counter to much of what we know about intrinsic motivation.

For administrators: Districts often purchase boxed programs because they're aligned with standards, are evidence-based, and offer overwhelmed teachers concrete materials and lessons. They also seem to offer consistency across a school or district. Some downsides to these programs are also revealed in some of their upsides. When consistency becomes sameness, when concrete materials and lessons lead to nonnegotiable inflexibility, students and teachers lose their autonomy, and there's often little room for curiosity or fun. When the goal of the work is about being compliant with the program—instead of the program being about supporting great teaching and learning—there's a problem.

FIGURE 6.1

Assume and Reinforce Intrinsic Motivation

	Instead of...	Try This...
Send positive messages about learning and school	"I know some of you don't like history, but..."	"We're going to explore some really interesting historical events today."
Indicate student ownership	"Here's what I want you to do in this next activity."	"Here's what you'll get to do in this next activity."
Emphasize student accomplishment over teacher approval	"I love the way you worked so carefully on today's lab!"	"You worked so carefully on today's lab!"
Offer realistic encouragement about effort	"You should always try your best—always give 100 percent!"	"See if you can focus and work hard for the next 20 minutes."

As you're looking for new curricula for your school or district, you might look for ones that will connect with students' (and teachers'!) intrinsic motivators. Is choice built into the program so that students and teachers can have some autonomy? Does the work students (and teachers) do feel real and authentic, or is it more worksheet and workbook driven? Look for programs and approaches that offer ideas to teachers without being scripted or overly lockstep.

For teachers: If you're not careful, scripted units and boxed curricula can stifle your creativity and diminish both teacher and student motivation. Although you may be required to use these materials, you can probably find small ways of elevating student voice and choice. For example, on a set of grammar exercises, students might get to choose the problems to solve that feel like the best level of challenge. Or in a writing unit on persuasion, you might say to the students, "Here's the topic the writing unit suggests. Can you think of others that might be fun to work on and still meet the same learning goals?" These are subtle but important shifts we can make to boost student autonomy (as well as our own), even in the midst of prescriptive programs. If you have more leeway, you might even replace whole units with your own while still teaching the core content of the units. For example, one year when using a prescriptive math program, I took all of the required standards for the geometry unit, taught lessons about those standards (some of which I borrowed or adjusted from the program), and then students got to design quilt squares that demonstrated all of the standards from the unit. We combined the quilt squares into a beautiful quilt to hang in our classroom.

❋ ❋ ❋

Are you eager to implement some of the ideas you've explored in this chapter? It can be helpful to begin with some self-reflection. What are you already doing? What are you doing a bit of but would like to strengthen? What are some next steps you might consider? Figure 6.2 is meant to be a starting point—an example you can use to plan your own self-reflection journey. Feel free to use it as is or change it however you like!

FIGURE 6.2

Instructional Strategies

	Yes	Somewhat	Not Yet
Choice: Students have many opportunities (simple and complex) to choose elements of their work: what they learn, how they learn, and how they demonstrate learning.			
Cocreation: Students have many opportunities to lend their voice to the planning process and to help design learning opportunities across content areas.			
Differentiated Learning: Student learning opportunities are diverse and can accommodate the varied needs, abilities, and preferences of all learners.			
Authentic: Students engage in real work that has purpose beyond a grade or completing an assignment.			

continued

FIGURE 6.2—(continued)
Instructional Strategies

	Yes	Somewhat	Not Yet
Culturally Responsive: Students can see themselves in their learning.			
Active and Interactive: Students spend more time engaged in work and talking than they do listening to someone else talk.			
Teacher Talk: You speak with students in ways that assume and promote intrinsic motivation about academic learning.			

Conclusion

It would be impossible for all lessons, activities, units, and learning experiences for students to connect with all six intrinsic motivators. However, a worthy goal might be to make sure that all learning activities for students connect with at least one (and preferably more) of them. If the work offers students some power and control, the chance to feel challenged and successful, some meaning, some fun, a sense of connection to others or a chance to connect with personal interests, students will be more inclined to have energy and enthusiasm for their learning.

There are so many wonderful books out there about great academic work. Here are a few to get you started if you'd like to explore this topic some more:

- *Empower: What Happens When Students Own Their Learning* by John Spencer and A. J. Juliani (2017)
- *The Teacher You Want to Be: Essays About Children, Learning, and Teaching* by Matt Glover and Ellin Oliver Keene (2015)
- *Learning to Choose, Choosing to Learn: The Key to Student Motivation and Achievement* by Mike Anderson (2016)

- *The Research-Ready Classroom: Differentiating Instruction Across Content Areas* by Mike Anderson and Andy Dousis (2006)
- *Students at the Center: Personalized Learning with Habits of Mind* by Bena Kallick and Allison Zmuda (2017)
- *Creating Cultures of Thinking: The 8 Forces We Must Master to Truly Transform Our Schools* by Ron Ritchhart (2015)
- *Motivation to Learn: Transforming Classroom Culture to Support Student Achievement* by Michael Middleton and Kevin Perks (2014)

7

Feedback and Assessment

What does it look like when we align our feedback and assessment practices with intrinsic motivation? This is an area that has seen a lot of change in schools over the past decade or so, but there's still a long way to go. Traditional school grading systems persist in many places—systems that were put in place for our previous goals for school, aligned with the need for compliance in the workplace. Instead of using feedback and grades to manage and motivate students' behaviors, we can offer students information to support their self-motivation. Instead of using grades to rank and sort students, we can individualize grades to help all students gain a sense of competence. Instead of assessment being primarily something teachers do to students' work, students can take on a more prominent role. Here are a few important shifts to consider if you'd like assessment and feedback practices to support students' intrinsic motivation.

Grades Are Competency-Based

As we have already discussed, traditional grading systems and structures can emphasize competition over collaboration and can reduce students' intrinsic motivation and learning. Competency-based grading, on the other hand, can help support students' intrinsic motivation.

In some systems, letter grades are still used, but grades are based on learning competencies (not in relation to how others perform). If the learning objectives are appropriate, the teacher teaches well, and students work hard, all students can demonstrate a high level of competence, and that can be reflected in their grades. All students getting good grades is then an indication of great teaching and learning instead of a lack of rigor. And, if all students are struggling with a concept, instead of scaling grades up to offer the façade that some have learned at a high level, we would expect the class to slow down, back up, and engage in some more learning—to make sure everyone actually learns the content. Wouldn't that be a better way to ensure and reflect high academic standards?

In other systems, letter grades aren't used at all. Instead of simply receiving a single score (a *C+*, for example) on an assignment, students receive feedback based on multiple competencies, reflecting that they were proficient in several items, partially proficient in one item, and not yet proficient in another. Without the judgment of the grade, students can focus instead on their learning and worry less about how they compare with others.

Self-Motivation Is Emphasized

In traditional systems, grades serve as both carrots and sticks. "In order to get an *A*, your work needs to be high-quality" or "If you don't want to lose points, you need to make sure to turn work in on time." Bonus points and extra credit are awarded for extra work, and zeros or point deductions are threatened for late or messy work. Grades are even used as motivators for nonacademic behaviors. My own two children in high school were offered bonus points for bringing in boxes of tissues and remembering to put their phones in the phone hotel by the classroom door. I know of other schools where students lose academic points for talking out of turn or coming in late to class. Although grades might be motivating (extrinsically) for some, it's not enough for many, so schools and parents add extra layers of rewards and punishments to the carrots and sticks of grades. In order to participate in sports, kids need to have all of their grades above a *D*. The ice cream social at the end of the month is available to students with a *C* average or above. Parents offer kids money for grades on their report cards and threaten to take away privileges if grades aren't high enough. Honor roll awards, National Honor Society recognition, and merit scholarships for college are further enticements to get good grades—added extrinsic motivators to reach for the extrinsic motivators. As we saw in Chapter 2, these are the very practices that pull the focus and attention of students away from the actual learning. Kids either don't care about grades, so they don't care about the work (because the work is justified by the grades), or they do care about the grades and see learning as a means to an end. This can lead to more linear and less creative thinking and even unethical behaviors like cheating.

We can dramatically shift this tone by creating work infused with intrinsic motivators (as we explored in the previous chapter) and then focusing feedback on students' learning and emphasizing intrinsic motivation. Instead of trying to motivate students' work ("Your draft needs more details if you want to get a good grade on the final paper"), we can assume that students want to do well and focus feedback on how to get there ("Some more details will help you more fully explain your reasoning in this paper"). We might also provide more formative in-process feedback to support students' ongoing growth and learning instead of focusing on summative feedback—judgments delivered after the work is finished. This doesn't mean that we don't want feedback to be motivational, by the way. Formative feedback is incredibly motivating, as it provides guidance and support to help students achieve their goals.

Assessments Are Varied

Another indication that grading is about comparing kids instead of assessing their learning in relation to learning goals is standardized grading practices. The belief is that in order to be fair (an indication that grades are about comparing kids), all kids need to be measured and graded in the same way. All students must take the same test. All students must experience the same scoring rubric. All students must have weights given to the same assignments and in the same proportions. Even though we know that some students are good test takers and others aren't, even though we know some students can show competence through speaking or active demonstration better than through essay writing, even though we know some students will need more or less time than others to gain true competence, all are given the same assessments. It's clear that the goal isn't simply to assess learning—it's about assessing learning in relation to others. This sets students up as competitors, reducing some students' sense of positive belonging and connection to peers.

Grading expert Thomas R. Guskey asks an uncomfortable question that also highlights the need for varied assessments: Is your primary goal when working with students to select talent or to develop it (2011)? If your goal is to select talent—to find the most talented students and raise them above others—then you should create assessments that highlight those differences. A classic example of this is to create a test that everyone will take with questions that only a few (the "top") students will be able to answer—questions that go way beyond the stated learning objectives. This will ensure that only a few students get high grades, and there will be greater variations between the scores of other students.

If your goal is to develop talent, however, then you work like crazy to teach and assess students in different ways. The goal isn't to separate the wheat from the chaff, it is to support all students in high-quality learning. Now, we might use many different assessments to better understand students' level of competence instead of relying on just one. For example, if the goal is for students to "describe the two-dimensional figures that result from slicing three-dimensional figures" (CCSS.MATH.CONTENT.7.G.A.3), students could "describe" their understanding through multiple-choice test questions, by creating their own drawings, through oral articulation, in writing, or in a combination of any of these.

I was observing a high school science class and saw a teacher offering choice and variety to her students in a summative assessment. She created a menu of options for how students could demonstrate mastery of the measurement skills they had been working on. I was walking around and talking with students and asking them about their choices. One student, Kyle, was adamant as he explained to me why he chose to use a meterstick to measure items around the room. He pointed with disgust at students working on more traditional test items. "I hate worksheets, but I like doing stuff with my hands." I related this mini conversation to his teacher, and she nodded and chuckled: "When Kyle ain't happy—ain't nobody happy!" Not only could Kyle better demonstrate his understanding of science skills through the hands-on option, but the rest of the class could better focus on their assessments because Kyle wasn't dysregulated.

There are a variety of ways students can demonstrate their understanding of content and their mastery of skills. They might do any of the following:

- Perform (deliver a speech, dance, play a piece of music, put on a skit, etc.)
- Demonstrate (solve a problem, read a passage, perform an experiment, etc.)
- Collect learning artifacts in a student portfolio
- Take a test or quiz
- Explain their understanding in a one-on-one conversation
- Write (an essay, blog series, poem, children's book, cartoon/comic series, etc.)
- Create and share a project (create a video or board game, design a poster, build a PowerPoint presentation, record a podcast, etc.)
- Generate their own ideas for how to demonstrate mastery

Students Play a Significant Role in Assessment

When it's viewed as the teacher's responsibility to be in charge of assessment, it's hard for work not to feel like an exercise in compliance. "Doing well" means meeting the teacher's demands. Imagine how energy might shift if students play a more significant role in assessment. Here are two ways to offer students more autonomy with assessment.

Student Goal Setting

Consider teaching students how to set authentic goals—ones that are personally meaningful and realistic—about their work. For example, let's say you're creating a checklist of writing skills and criteria for an upcoming writing workshop. The unit is an exploration of narrative writing, so you begin by listing the competencies connected with narrative writing from your standards. Next, you could have students add a few of their own goals. What are the skills they want to focus on? In addition to skills like "Provide a conclusion that follows from the narrated experiences or events" (CCSS.

ELA.LITERACY.W.5.3.E), kids could add goals like "Write a story that's at least five pages long" or "Add detailed illustrations that support my story." Imagine how much more motivational that might be for students.

Student-Designed Self-Assessments

So often, assessments—both the assessments themselves and the criteria and objectives that are being assessed—feel devoid of life and energy and completely removed from what kids really care about. I haven't met a kid yet who really cared about how well they can "present claims and findings, sequencing ideas logically and using pertinent descriptions, facts, and details to accentuate main ideas or themes" (which is, by the way, only *part* of standard ELA-Literacy.SL.6.4 of the Common Core State Standards). It's fine that these standards inform our teaching and students' learning, but what if some of the time we let students design their own assessments about the things they care about?

We can tap into students' need for autonomy and strengthen their sense of purpose by having them generate some of their own self-assessments. In one 6th grade class in Massachusetts, the class had generated a bunch of ideas for how to learn key math vocabulary words. Students then chose the method that seemed best to them. Some students created crossword puzzles for classmates to solve, a few designed simple visuals that showed artistic renderings of words, and two students wrote and read aloud scripts for a talk show interview (on the talk show *Meet That Number!*), where they embedded the math vocabulary words within the context of the interviews. The teacher then asked the class for ideas about criteria they should all pay attention to, regardless of the method they chose. Through a class discussion, the students decided to self-assess using a check, check-plus, and check-minus rating scale in three categories: effective use of the words, level of polish, and creativity. The teacher told me that he was blown away by how thoughtful and honest students were with their self-assessments.

Once again, consider the rich opportunities for skill building that this kind of teaching offers. Students can learn and practice skills of metacognition, self-reflection, self-awareness, and many other emotional competencies.

Feedback Is Strengths-Based

In order for feedback to support self-motivation, it has to build students' sense of competence, not break it down. Feedback that focuses on what students are lacking or the mistakes students have made can cripple motivation. That doesn't mean that feedback can't be critical—it just means that we should be thoughtful about the amount of critical feedback students receive, as well as the tone of it.

Feedback That Emphasizes Student Strengths

Let's first consider a few ways to emphasize students' strengths through feedback. Often, simple shifts can make a big difference.

Mark what's right instead of what's wrong. When correcting something with clear right and wrong answers such as a math paper, a vocabulary assignment, or a science quiz, instead of marking the wrong answers (especially with a big X in red pen!), mark the ones that are correct.

Be specific. Instead of offering general feedback such as "Good writing," "Great job!" or "Awesome thinking," give more specific details about what students did well. For example, instead of saying, "Great reading!" after a student has read aloud a passage in a reading conference, you might say, "Your reading was really smooth, and your voice changed to match the tone of the story as you read!"

Emphasize learning over talent. The work of Carol Dweck (2006) has made it clear that offering students feedback that focuses on talent or intelligence ("You're so smart!") can put students in a fixed mindset where they'll be less likely to take risks in the future. Instead, in addition to being more specific with feedback, we can emphasize effort and learning: "You worked so hard on science lab, and it really paid off. Your analysis was crisp and concise while still including all of the important information you needed!"

Feedback That Supports Competence

Feedback that helps you grow is also motivational, if it's done well. It strengthens your sense of growth and learning. Let's consider a few ideas for how to offer critical feedback in a way that will support motivation.

Frame critiques in terms of growth. Instead of framing critiques as negatives (weaknesses, problems, mistakes), use terms that imply growth and learning (next steps, pushes, goals, areas for growth). Imagine how much more competent you would feel when getting feedback about a lesson you had taught if instead of hearing, "Here are two weaknesses of this lesson..." you heard, "Here are two ideas to try next time...."

Keep critiques manageable. If we give students too many suggestions at once, they're likely going to feel overwhelmed, and this can lead students to shut down and give up. Instead, offer one or two suggestions at a time, and keep the suggestions within the abilities of the student—something they can reasonably tackle with success.

Offer constructive feedback while work is in process, not when it's finished. Once work is finished, criticisms don't do students much good because it's too late to use them to improve their work. Instead, offer suggestions for improvement while students still have a chance to try them. Once work is finished, focus on celebrating accomplishments and learning.

FAQ: Don't colleges require traditional grades?

A common concern about moving away from traditional grading systems is that colleges use grades for admissions. Won't students be disadvantaged if their transcript isn't traditional? The good news is the answer is a clear no.

For one thing, colleges know that high schools are all different and their transcripts (even the ones using traditional grades) aren't consistent. Admissions staff know that they need to look at high school profiles to understand how individual schools' transcripts work. For example, some schools' letter grades correspond with even 10-point ranges (an average of 90–100 is an *A*, 80–89 is a *B*, 70–79 is a *C*, etc.) while other schools have a tighter range (93–100 is an *A*, 85–92 is a *B*, 75–84 is a *C*, 70–74 is a *D*). Colleges also receive transcripts from international schools, nontraditional schools, nongraded schools, and students who have been homeschooled.

Colleges are also acknowledging the movement toward proficiency-based grading systems. In 2016, the New England Board of Higher Education published a white paper that detailed feedback from college and university admissions leaders from across New England. Not only did these admissions officers overwhelmingly state that proficiency-based transcripts wouldn't hurt students' admission chances to their schools, some admissions leaders also said that "features of the proficiency-based transcript model...provide important information for institutions seeking not just high-performing academics, but engaged, life-long learners" (Blauth & Hadjian, 2016). The New England Secondary School Consortium has listed 85 New England colleges and universities that have provided statements and letters stating that "students with proficiency-based grades and transcripts will not be disadvantaged in any way." Some of the most elite colleges and universities in the United States are listed among these schools, including Amherst, Bates, Bowdoin, Brown, Colby, Connecticut College, Dartmouth, Massachusetts Institute of Technology, Middlebury, Trinity, Tufts, Wellesley, Williams, and Yale, as well as the Universities of Connecticut, Maine, Massachusetts, New Hampshire, Rhode Island, and Vermont (New England Secondary School Consortium, n.d.).

With all of the anxiety surrounding the college admissions process, it can feel like colleges and universities are looking for ways to exclude kids from their schools, but this isn't the norm. Having just gone through the college admissions process with both of my children, I can assure you that colleges and universities want to admit kids to their schools. They're looking for every possible way to figure out which kids will be good fits in their schools, and they're not going to let proficiency-based transcripts, which often provide more, not less, information about a child's academic performance, get in their way.

FAQ: Would we be better off with no grades at all?

We might be, but here is another answer that is a bit nuanced. Traditional grading systems are limiting, provide too little information, and are too easily turned into incentives—which then lead to many of the negative outcomes we explored in Chapter 2. However, grades that provide information to support students' sense of competence and strengthen the purpose of learning can be vehicles for supporting self-motivation.

Here is one example. In an article in *Educational Leadership,* Daniel Venables shares the story of a colleague who managed to pull this off with traditional grades. This teacher was legendary for his ability to teach 9th graders how to write. In his class, there were three grades you could get on an any assignment: *A, B,* or *Not Yet.* Anything that did not reach the criteria for an *A* or *B* was deemed not ready and needed more work. Work had to be proficient—it had to meet the standard—in order to be complete. In this class, the goal was competency, and the grade indicated that you accomplished the goal (2020).

On the other hand, it might be worth considering getting rid of grades altogether. Many teachers are. Mark Barnes and Starr Sackstein are teachers and authors who have written about this extensively. They help moderate a Facebook group called "Teachers Throwing Out Grades" whose mission (according to the "About" section of their group) is "dedicated to eliminating traditional grades and making learning a conversation that involves education's most important shareholders—students" (Teachers Throwing Out Grades, n.d.). As of the writing of this book, the group had well over 11,000 members.

* * *

Are you eager to implement some of the ideas you've explored in this chapter? It can be helpful to begin with some self-reflection. What are you already doing? What are you doing a bit of but would like to strengthen? What are some next steps you might consider? Figure 7.1 is meant to be a starting point—an example you can use to plan your own self-reflection journey. Feel free to use it as is or change it however you like!

Conclusion

As an individual teacher who has limited power over the grading systems of your school or district, this doesn't need to feel overwhelming. Choose one or two things to work at to shift how assessment and feedback feel for your students. Even if you need to give official traditional letter grades, you can assess and emphasize competencies met in your daily feedback. You can shift the way you talk about the relationship between learning and grades,

FIGURE 7.1

Assessment and Feedback

	Yes	Somewhat	Not Yet
Competency-Based: Assessments focus on students' learning of content and skills—not on points or grades.			
Self-Assessment: In addition to teacher-created assessments, students have many opportunities to reflect on and self-assess their own work and learning.			
Student Goal Setting: In addition to working toward curricular competencies, students are supported in setting their own goals for learning.			
Varied: Students have many ways to demonstrate learning and competencies. One-size-fits-all assessments are not used as the sole determination of learning.			
Ongoing: Students can demonstrate learning at various times—not just during a one-time event. Speed of learning, or learning something in one try, is not valued.			
Strengths-Based: Feedback is more focused on what students can do and what they have accomplished than on deficiencies.			
Specific: Feedback is specific—helping students understand strengths and next steps in their learning.			
Self-Motivation: The primary role of assessment and feedback is to provide students with information to fuel their self-motivation.			

emphasizing that the grades should help lead to better learning instead of learning being about getting good grades. You might experiment a little with self-assessment, helping your students to become more reflective and self-aware, sharing some of the power and control of feedback with them.

For additional reflection about competency- and proficiency-based grading, check out these resources:

- *Assessing with Respect: Everyday Practices That Meet Students' Social and Emotional Needs* by Starr Sackstein (2021)
- *Grading Smarter, Not Harder: Assessment Strategies That Motivate Kids and Help Them Learn* by Myron Dueck (2014)
- *Rethinking Grading: Meaningful Assessment for Standards-Based Learning* by Cathy Vatterott (2015)
- *Charting a Course to Standards-Based Grading: What to Stop, What to Start, and Why It Matters* by Tim R. Westerberg (2016)
- *What We Know About Grading: What Works, What Doesn't, and What's Next* by Thomas R. Guskey and Susan M. Brookhart (2019)

8

Discipline and Classroom Management

Too often in schools—even if the academic work is rich and fascinating and taps into many intrinsic motivators—the discipline system and classroom management strategies still focus on rote compliance. So what would it look like if autonomy, belonging, competence, purpose, fun, and curiosity helped shape the way we approach discipline in the classroom?

Foundational Beliefs About Discipline

Before we get to specific practices and strategies, there are a few important ideas that we should be clear about—foundational beliefs about the teaching of discipline that are key to the effectiveness of the practices and strategies that follow.

- **Kids do well if they can.** This is a mantra made popular by clinical child psychologist Ross Greene, who has done incredible work in the United States and internationally to support children who struggle with emotional regulation. He makes it clear that challenging behaviors aren't about kids not wanting to do well—they're about kids not being able to meet the expectations of the moment. Once we understand this, we realize that we should stop trying to motivate students' behavior and instead give them the skills and strategies needed to be successful. They already want to do well, and incentive systems only make things worse.

- **We need to teach discipline.** As Ruth Charney pointed out in her iconic book about discipline, *Teaching Children to Care,* "The word discipline is derived from the Latin root *disciplina* meaning learning" (2002, p. 19). Discipline is something children learn. That means that discipline is something teachers must teach. There is a rich array of self-management and social interaction skills that you can help your students learn that will serve them well now, while they're in school, and later, once they have moved on.

- **We should focus more time and energy on proactive than on reactive strategies.** Students won't learn to be great spellers simply by having their spelling mistakes circled. The same holds true for discipline. Though consequences are a necessary part of an effective approach to discipline, it's the proactive teaching of discipline that will be most helpful for children.

- **Discipline and academic work go hand in hand.** It's hard to imagine students being able to engage in active and interactive learning without skills of self-control, persistence, cooperation, empathy, and effective decision making. Similarly, how could children ever practice skills like this in the absence of great academic work? We must teach skills of discipline in the midst of great academic work and design great academic work to facilitate prosocial and emotional skill development.

- **Relationships are at the heart of discipline.** Building strong connections with students is critically important to effective discipline. We must take the time to really get to know our students and to earn their trust and respect in order to engage in the hard work of helping them become more disciplined.

- **Rewards should be internal.** Kids should feel good when they share with others, show responsibility, work hard, and help each other out. This means that we should not impose external rewards for behaviors because these systems typically lower intrinsic motivation.

- **Discipline is equitable.** Adults are vigilant about ensuring that all students of all genders, ethnicities, socioeconomic backgrounds, and so on are treated fairly. When inequities appear, action is taken.

The following practices and strategies are ones that will help you align your classroom management with your goal of helping students develop more self-motivation. As you explore these ideas, consider the many connections you see to students' intrinsic drives for autonomy, belonging, competence, purpose, fun, and curiosity. Each of these strategies is explained in enough depth to get you started, but each could practically be its own book. In light of this, I have included suggestions for further reading at the end of this chapter.

Cocreation of Norms and Rules

In a classroom where the discipline system is modeled on the industrial-age workplace, the rules likely come from above. Teachers make the rules, and kids' job is to follow them. Obedience and compliance are the goals, and students usually feel little autonomy or sense of purpose about the guiding norms of the room. Instead, we can cocreate working norms with our students to elevate their voices, connect with their sense of purpose, and boost their sense of belonging.

Invest time early in the year in helping students create the rules of the class. The following steps are general and can be used and adapted to fit just about any grade and age.

1. **Envision an ideal learning environment.** What do students hope to learn? How do they want the class to feel? Have students articulate and share these ideas with each other to help them both hear a diversity of perspectives and find some common themes.
2. **Generate a list of possible norms.** If the goal is to reach for an ideal learning environment (Step 1), how should people treat each other? How should people talk with each other? How will everyone care for themselves and the learning environment? It's important to connect

Steps 1 and 2. The rules for the class (what we'll do) should flow from our shared sense of purpose (why we care).

3. **Narrow the list down to a few.** Look for themes and categories that seem to go together. You might have a class discussion to do this, have students discuss ideas in small groups, or if you teach younger children, you might do this part yourself. Try to capture all of the ideas in the big list within just a few broad rules (e.g., be nice to others, don't swear, share supplies, help each other when we're stuck, and don't say mean things could all fit under the global rule "Respect others").

4. **Gain consensus.** Keep playing with the wording of the rules until you have class consensus. That means everyone agrees that the rules will help guide the class toward building the ideal environment they envisioned in Step 1.

Now that the class norms are complete, you can post them so they're easy to see. I used to leave a space for students to sign the rules. Signing the rules was voluntary (though in 15 years, I never had a student not sign them), and it meant that the students agreed that the rules would help us as a class. Signing was *not* a promise to follow them all of the time. After all, we're all going to make mistakes!

Cocreation of Routines

Just as we can cocreate rules with students, we can also invite them to help us figure out some of the routines. Although some routines we can simply model and practice, there are certainly ones we can have students help shape. See Figure 8.1 for some examples.

Think about the message students receive about their level of autonomy when they are asked for their ideas about how to structure even simple routines. They start to feel a sense of shared belonging and ownership in the room—it's theirs, not just ours. Try eliciting ideas from students (see pp. 90–91) to elevate students' voices so they can help craft the routines of the room.

FIGURE 8.1

Routines We Might Cocreate with Students

Grades PreK–1	Grades 2–5	Grades 6–8	Grades 9–12
• Different positions to use when sitting in circle • Games to play at morning meeting • Which songs to play for clean-up transitions	• Where students will line up to leave room • How to display names on online platform • Bathroom sign-out procedures • Class jobs and how they're designated	• Transitioning through halls (when going to lockers, restrooms, etc.) • Placement of materials in room for easy access • System for passing in work • How to raise your hand in an online discussion	• How to settle in for class (a minute or two to chat, get settled and ready) • Arrangement of furniture for discussions or group activities • Roles for collaborative groups (in person or online)

We can also be open to student suggestions with routines we have established. Here's a quick example. Recently, I was teaching a demonstration lesson in a 6th grade classroom. I taught the group how I would use a raised hand as a signal that they should wrap up partner chats soon (but not immediately). Students were standing in concentric circles as they discussed the open-ended questions I had posed. After one round, a girl raised her hand and said, "When my back is to you, I can't see your hand." So I asked the group, "Hmmm. Anyone have an idea for how we could adjust the signal?" One student said, "You could count down so we could hear the signal, too." I responded, "Let's try it, but I'm going to count down quietly, since I don't want to overpower you with my voice, and I don't want to cut you off mid-sentence as you're talking." We tried that in the next round, and I asked the students, "How did that work? Was that helpful?" They agreed that it was, so I kept using that quiet countdown from five along with the hand signal. It was clear from students' reactions—their facial expressions and body language—that they felt empowered and validated with this shift.

This brings up another important point about routines of the room. That signal I just shared is one that allows students some self-control. They need to self-regulate in order to wrap up conversations before being ready to listen. Some signals are more about controlling students, such as when the teacher rings a bell and all students are supposed to freeze or the teacher claps and the students are supposed to clap back. These signals reinforce compliance and obedience and send the clear message that the teacher's need for attention is more important than the students' needs to finish their thought, which diminishes students' sense of autonomy. I encourage you to examine the routines in your classroom. Are there any that emphasize rigid conformity and compliance? How might you tweak them to share power and control with students?

Consequences

Consequences are tricky. On the one hand, it's hard to imagine an effective approach to discipline without them. They lend structure and limits to discipline. Like the guardrails on a highway, they help keep accidents from getting worse. As a child starts to scribble on someone else's paper, we take away their crayon and move their seat. What could have been a full-blown fight was contained. And just as guardrails don't build driving skills, consequences alone don't do much for development of self-regulation or responsibility. So we should use consequences as needed to set limits and to keep bad things from getting worse, but they should not be the focus or emphasis of an approach to discipline. When we spend lots of time looking for the "right" consequence to fix the problem, we know we've veered back into the territory of using consequences to motivate behavior.

Natural Consequences

Sometimes, consequences are natural—all adults need to do is let them happen. If children don't bring their jackets out for recess, they get cold. If they forget their violin, they don't have an instrument to play during orchestra rehearsal. As long as the consequence isn't too severe (e.g., we shouldn't let a child climb to the top of the swing set, because a broken limb—or worse—is too severe a consequence), we can just let it happen. Responding with empathy (a tone of genuine understanding—not an "I told you so" one) can let the child know we feel badly about what happened: "That's a bummer that you can't play your instrument today. How about we figure out a strategy to help you remember for next time?"

Logical Consequences

According to Jane Nelson in *Positive Discipline,* consequences are logical if they are *related* to what has happened, *respectful* of children and adults, *reasonable* from the child's and adult's perspective, and *revealed in advance*—meaning it's not a surprise for the child when it happens (2006, p. 107). Let's say a student isn't paying attention as he walks through the room, and he bumps into a stack of books, knocking them to the floor. A logical consequence would be to have him pick the books back up and put them in a neat stack—the way they were before he bumped them. This is clearly *related* to what happened. It's *respectful* as long as it's delivered in a matter-of-fact way ("Josh, make sure to pick the books back up and stack them neatly") without anger or sarcasm. It's certainly *reasonable* because it should only take a moment or two. Now the question is, was it *revealed in advance?* In my experience, it's not possible to reveal every possible logical consequence in advance because there are just too many possibilities. We also wouldn't want to always reveal possible consequences before engaging in activities around the room ("Remember everyone...if you're careless as you walk around, you're going to have to pick things up!"). This will sound like nagging or could even feel threatening. Instead, I recommend spending time early on with the class talking about consequences in general and how they're a part of how we hold ourselves responsible to the rules we've created. You might share some examples of possible consequences and even have the class brainstorm some ideas together. This helps set a tone of respectfulness about discipline and helps kids know how consequences work before we need to use them.

Social and Emotional Skills

Once we move away from expecting compliance—and punishing and rewarding our way there—it becomes imperative that we teach children the skills they need to be successful. It's not enough to say to a group, "You all need to work together, so cooperate!" That would be like handing a kid a trumpet and saying, "Play!" Instead, we need to help students learn the skills needed for sharing ideas, listening to each other, cooling off when they're upset, taking turns in a discussion, and compromising. Kids need direct instruction, time to reflect, and opportunities to practice social and emotional skills just like they do with academic ones.

There's a common mistake I see happening in schools that I want to warn you about. Social and emotional skills need to be taught and practiced within the context of real work. We should offer students strategies for cooperative group work as they're working in groups. We should model skills involved in an effective writing conference during writing—as kids are about to confer. We shouldn't try to teach social and emotional learning as a separate content area at a designated time. It's the old assembly-line mentality: We teach math from 8:00 to 9:00, social studies from 9:00 to 10:00, and social-emotional learning from 10:00 to 10:30. This is like trying to teach someone a new serve in tennis when they're not on the court. How well will the lesson stick without a chance to practice and receive coaching right away? If your district has purchased kits for social-emotional learning, see if you can mine them for lessons to use throughout your teaching instead of teaching stand-alone lessons devoid of context.

Of course, the reason that schools purchase kits and stand-alone curricula is that it can be overwhelming to teach something as complex as social-emotional learning without some support and guidance. Here's an activity to try that will help your teaching of SEL be more authentic and contextual. First, grab a copy of the social-emotional skills targets your district has adopted. (If your district hasn't adopted anything, I recommend one of two other resources: either the set created by CASEL (https://casel.org/core-competencies/) or the Habits of Mind (www.habitsofmindinstitute.org/what-are-habits-of-mind/).) Next, take a look at an upcoming unit that you're just about to teach. Try a scavenger hunt. Search through the unit to see which social-emotional skills your students might need to be successful with their academic work. Then, weave some small moments of teaching (using either effective modeling or eliciting ideas from students; see pp. 89–91) right into your academic lessons.

Teacher Talk

Another aspect of management and discipline to examine is the way we talk to and with students about behavior. Are we using language habits that reinforce students' feelings of autonomy, belonging, competence, and purpose, or are we accidentally emphasizing obedience and compliance to teacher demands? Check out Figure 8.2 for a few examples to consider.

FIGURE 8.2 **Rethink Praise**	
Instead of Emphasizing Teacher Pleasing and Compliance	**Focus on What Students Have Done and Why It's Positive**
"I love the way you cleaned up so well after that last activity!"	"You got everything cleaned up—that was really responsible!"
"Great job working so well together as a team!"	"You're really working well as a team!"
"I'm so proud of the way you're all taking turns in your breakout group!"	"You're all taking turns well in the breakout group. That's helping all voices be heard!"
"I like how you stayed focused for the whole writing period today!"	"You stayed focused for the whole writing period today! What helped you stay so focused?"

Use language that's higher on the moral hierarchy to emphasize the class rules that you've created with students and higher moral principles. Move away from language that emphasizes punishments, rewards, and approval. These are language habits that are about compliance instead of belonging, autonomy, and purpose (see Figure 8.3).

Flexible Seating

During work periods, when students are working independently or in small groups, instead of assigning seats and requiring all students to sit in the same way, we can offer a variety of seating options. Some students might want to sit at tables, while others might prefer to stand at a counter. Some

FIGURE 8.3

Explaining Why Assignments Should Be Turned In On Time

Instead of...	Try This...
"I'd love it if you could turn assignments in on time."	"When you turn in assignments on time, you show responsibility to yourself and respect for others."
"If you can turn assignments in on time, you'll get full credit and a higher grade."	"You can work toward our rule about responsibility by handing in assignments on time."
"If you turn in assignments late, I'll contact your parents, and there will be negative consequences."	"Turning your homework in on time gives us both a chance to make sure you're on track with learning before we move on to the next concept."

might want to sit on the floor with a few peers, while others might do better in a desk on their own. This simple strategy is one more way we can boost student autonomy.

Class Meetings

When class issues arise, or a class decision needs to be made, students can participate in a class meeting to discuss ideas and come to consensus, which strengthens their sense of belonging. Help students gain consensus on solutions, and then help them follow through on their decisions. Consider having a notebook or shared online document for everyone to access where students can sign up to bring issues up for a class meeting. With some practice, older students can eventually lead and facilitate their own meetings.

Collaborative Problem Solving

When students are struggling with ongoing issues, either with schoolwork or behavior, teachers can work with students to help them uncover and try possible solutions. Teachers can help students identify the root cause of the problem and then, together, they can come up with ideas to try. When done well, in addition to empowering students and boosting their sense of competence, this practice also strengthens relationships between teacher and student, and students see teachers as allies who help them solve tough problems.

FAQ: What about children with challenging behaviors?

As was mentioned at the beginning of this chapter, academic work goes hand in hand with discipline. It's hard to have self-regulated students in the absence of compelling work. Yet too often in schools, children who exhibit challenging behaviors (who, not surprisingly, also often struggle academically) are separated from the regular classrooms (diminishing their sense of belonging), put in low-ability groups (diminishing their already low sense of competence), and spoon-fed skill building activities that are often devoid of any purpose (from the perspective of the child). In fact, children with emotional and behavioral disorders benefit immensely from choice (Jolivette, Stichter, & McCormick, 2002). Offering students choices about their academics has been shown to boost student accuracy as well as task completion (Cosden, Gannon, & Haring, 1995) and decrease disruptive behavior (Dunlap et al., 1994). What if, instead of offering students who struggle less engaging academic work, we offered them more of it? And of course, we'll need to teach students the many social and emotional skills they'll need to handle this rich and meaningful work successfully.

FAQ: Should incentives ever be used for students with extreme behaviors?

Michael McSheehan has spent decades working with children with significant intellectual and developmental disabilities. A leader in education and systems change, he has had extensive experience helping schools and districts across the United States implement approaches such as Multi-Tiered System of Support (MTSS), Positive Behavioral Interventions and Supports (PBIS), and Response to Intervention (RTI).

I posed this question to him, and he told the story of a boy (we'll call him Luke) he worked with the previous school year who was having a terrible time at school. He was constantly dysregulated, frequently disrupted class, and didn't do much (if any) schoolwork. His educational team attempted a variety of ways to support him through his meltdowns, which often put him or others at risk of harm. The often-used consequence of sending him home just made matters worse because he was so unhappy at school that he didn't want to stay, and his home was an unpredictable and traumatic environment.

"We tried everything we could that was in the context of the capacities of that school to proceed with strategies of intrinsic motivation," Michael explained. "But, even with the dedication and well-intentioned efforts of educators, the school didn't have the capacity to support this student in this way." Later in the conversation, he related that he thought that this child was experiencing further trauma because of his constant failures and out-of-control behaviors in school.

With the hope of getting this student out of crisis mode while also providing opportunities for learning, his educational team eventually explored alternative settings for him. They found one where the class sizes were small (with a maximum of eight students per room), the staff were highly trained in terms of Luke's specific needs, isolation rooms were not used, and there was a (new) clear and consistent message given to Luke: *You're never going home because of something that happens at school. We will get through it together.* There was also a token economy system where Luke could earn (but never lose) points (that could be traded in for various items on the prize shelves) for successful school behaviors. So far, Luke has been experiencing never-before-seen success at this new school.

So he concluded that, in extreme circumstances, when used by highly skilled people, and as a part of a broader system of support, a token economy system might be appropriate for a period of time in a child's education. "Although," Michael concluded with concern, "if Luke experiences tokens right through high school, he'll never be able to function outside of school."

FAQ: I'm in a school that uses a token economy incentive system, but I don't want to. What should I do?

This is hard. On the one hand, you want to support your school's goals and be in line with your colleagues, and you know that consistency with either discipline or academic practices is important for students. On the other hand, once you understand the potential downsides to incentive systems, it can be troubling to still use these practices with your students. There's no one right way to go here, but there are some ideas you might try.

Can you share your conflicted feelings with your students in a way that they can understand and that doesn't undermine your colleagues? For example, you might say to a group of older students, "I know you're all excited about the Star Reward program in our school, and I want you to be able to participate. On the other hand, I don't want you to worry so much about getting stars that you lose sight of doing the right things for the right reasons." Perhaps you could then ask for their advice. "How can we still participate in the program without it becoming too much of a focus?" Could you even let your students give themselves stars when they feel they've met the criteria? You might set a limit of a certain number of stars per day if you think a few students might have a hard time limiting themselves.

You could also continue to build intrinsic motivators into daily work and support students' skills of self-regulation, even if you still need to give them stars. Make sure the work is worth doing (from students' perspectives) and give them the skills they need to be successful. Then, when you do give students stars, keep it mellow and relaxed. Focus on what the student did ("You picked up some trash on the floor even though it wasn't yours") instead of the star ("Good job picking up trash—here's a star!").

Finally, you might gently open up conversations with colleagues about the system your school is using. Ask others how they feel about it. See if any others share your concerns. Find out if people have a common understanding of what it means if the system is "working." Is the system working if it allows teachers to manage students in the moment, or is it working if students are gaining the ability to manage themselves?

✳ ✳ ✳

Are you eager to implement some of the ideas you've explored in this chapter? It can be helpful to begin with some self-reflection. What are you already doing? What are you doing a bit of but would like to strengthen? What are some next steps you might consider? Figure 8.4 is meant to be a starting point—an example you can use to plan your own self-reflection journey. Feel free to use it as is or change it however you like!

FIGURE 8.4

Discipline

	Yes	Somewhat	Not Yet
Cocreation of Rules: You and your students collaborate to create respectful and realistic rules to support positive learning communities.			
Cocreation of Routines: You and your students collaborate to set up and practice routines that will allow for student independence.			
Respectful Consequences: Logical and natural consequences support learning but are not used to punish or to motivate behavior.			
Taught Skills: An emphasis is placed on proactive and intentional teaching of social and emotional skills students need to be successful in school.			
Internal Rewards: Students feel good when they are successful. Reward systems are not used.			
Equitable Discipline: You are vigilant about ensuring that all students—all genders, ethnicities, socioeconomic backgrounds, and so on—are treated fairly. When inequities appear, action is taken.			
Teacher Talk: You speak with students in ways that assume and support positive and internal motivation about self-management.			

Conclusion

As you reflect on the classroom management and discipline systems and strategies that you and your school use, it is important to consider whether they reflect the goals and values of the world we're moving into or the ones of the past. Decades ago, systems that reinforced compliance and obedience might have made a lot of sense because so many jobs and professions were built along similar structures. Workers were managed by managers, managers were managed by other managers, and only a very few people rose to the position where autonomy and self-management were required. This is simply no longer the case.

If we want to help raise children who are ready to be successful during and after their school experience, it's time to stop focusing on managing kids' behavior and instead help them to learn to manage themselves.

For additional reflection about effective discipline, check out these resources:

- *What We Say and How We Say It Matter: Teacher Talk That Improves Student Learning and Behavior* by Mike Anderson (2019)
- *Teaching Children to Care: Classroom Management for Ethical and Academic Growth, K–8* by Ruth Charney (2002)
- *The Explosive Child: A New Approach for Understanding and Parenting Easily Frustrated, Chronically Inflexible Children* by Ross Greene (2014)
- *Rules in School: Teaching Discipline in the Responsive Classroom* by Kathryn Brady, Mary Beth Forton, and Deborah Porter (2011)
- *Discipline with Dignity: How to Build Responsibility, Relationships, and Respect in Your Classroom* by Richard L. Curwin, Allen N. Mendler, and Brian D. Mendler (2018)
- *Hanging In: Strategies for Teaching the Students Who Challenge Us Most* by Jeffrey Benson (2014)
- *Positive Discipline: The Classic Guide to Helping Children Develop Self-Discipline, Responsibility, Cooperation, and Problem-Solving Skills* by Jane Nelson (2006)
- *Better Than Carrots or Sticks: Restorative Practices for Positive Classroom Management* by Dominique Smith, Douglas Fisher, and Nancy Frey (2015)

9

Moving Away from Incentive Systems

You're in. You're excited about the idea of weaving more intrinsic motivators into students' learning, and you love the idea of not having to manage the "caught you being good" tickets and the Friday prize box. You're also excited to teach students skills of self-management. But where do you start?

My first recommendation is to not take on too much all at once. This will be overwhelming, and if you're already in the middle of the school year, it will probably be overwhelming for your students as well. Instead, try taking on some small changes, working to make the shift a bit at a time. Remember to be patient. You should expect an adjustment period, especially if you work with students who have experienced many different incentive systems over many years. Look for moments of growth over time, and give yourself permission not to rush or expect children to adjust to a new paradigm right away.

My second recommendation is to remember the complexity of motivation. You won't be able to stop dropping marbles in a jar or stop giving grades and substitute that with one other strategy. Instead, you'll need to think a bit more broadly. How can you boost intrinsic motivation just a bit in a given lesson or unit? What are some systems of extrinsic motivation that are in place that you can shift or deemphasize? Which self-management skills might students need to be successful, and how can you weave the teaching of those skills into what you're already doing?

141

Identify What Is Going Well and Then Transfer It

Chances are, you've already got some great things going on in your teaching. Can you take what's working well in one setting and transfer it to another?

Which lessons, activities, units, or classes do kids especially enjoy? When are they already excited and motivated about learning? Once you have identified a time when students are energized and motivated, make connections to the intrinsic motivators. Which ones are especially strong during these times?

For example, perhaps students love the science unit you're currently working on because there is a lot of hands-on work (fun), the topic is especially interesting (curiosity), and students are getting to work on demonstrations of their choice (autonomy) with a partner (belonging). Or maybe it's your sculpture class, where students are creating freestanding three-dimensional pieces out of repeated shapes from recycled material. It's really hard, but students see themselves making progress (competence). There is a lot of leeway within the parameters of the project (autonomy), and students are excited to share their creations in the display case in the front of the school when they're finished (belonging and purpose).

Once you have identified what's working in one area, consider how you might transfer it to another. For example, elementary school teachers often say that morning meeting is one of the most successful times of the day. Even with classes that are especially challenging, morning meetings are often a bright spot. Not surprisingly, they are often flush with intrinsic motivators. When students get to greet and share with each other, there's a strong sense of belonging. Games and activities, many of which connect with academic content, can be both fun and purposeful. This is also a time of day when all children can be successful, so kids are less likely to feel incompetent and slide into fight, flight, or freeze mode. Consider how many of these elements can be used during other parts of the day. There are plenty of collaborative games to play during academic periods that will foster a sense of positive connection with classmates as well as infuse some fun into learning. Students can use the same structures they learned at morning meeting to confer during writing workshop and math, share about books during reading, and generate ideas in science and social studies.

Perhaps reading workshop is another successful time. Students get to choose books (autonomy) that they can read independently (competence) and that they're interested in (curiosity). They share about their reading with peers (belonging) and create mini projects to share about their books with others (purpose). How might some of those same structures transfer to math? Perhaps students can choose problems to work on that are at their just-right math level (competence), have a chance to confer and share with each other (belonging), and create mini projects to showcase strategies they're using on a bulletin board in the classroom (purpose).

Ditch the Incentives, but Keep the Fun Stuff

When I decided to move away from giving students chips for good behavior and work, I knew they would be really upset to lose the chance to go to pizza for lunch. Quite frankly, I would, too. I loved going to lunch with a small group of students! I wanted to find a way to keep the good part of the system while getting rid of the part I had grown away from. So I ditched the chips and kept the pizza. I explained to my students that I was worried about how the chips seemed to be getting in the way: People were too worried about them, and they seemed to be damaging our classroom community. Then I explained that every Wednesday was going to be a pizza day, and one group of students would join me for lunch. I set up a rotating schedule, so with six groups in the room, every student got to go out for pizza every six weeks. I then spent more time teaching positive behaviors and reminding students as needed instead of relying on the chips to manage the class. It made a dramatic difference in the tone of the room.

Could this work for you? If you're currently giving students stickers if they have a good remedial reading group time, try simply giving students a sticker at the end of the session, whether they did well or not. Instead of using the sticker to get students to do what they should, make the work as engaging as possible, set them up for success with the skills they need (social and emotional as well as academic), and hand everyone a sticker on their way out of the door.

I was working with a K–2 school, and teachers were really worried about giving up their gem jars. For young children, seeing good deeds and positive moments pile up in the form of marbles or gems in a jar can be a concrete way for them to see their successes. My suggestion was to keep using the gem jars to notice positive behaviors but not have parties tied to filling the jars. Instead, when the jar is full, teachers could say, "Wow! Look at all of the good things we've accomplished! Let's see if we can fill it up again!" And of course, I recommended that they still have occasional pajama parties and fun movies—because they're fun!

How might this work with grades? Let's say your current practice is to correct tests by putting points next to each answer, with the total points tallying to 100 so the test can be given a corresponding letter grade. Instead, you could mark each problem with a note to show whether it met the standard, partially met the standard, or didn't meet the standard. These could be numbers such as 3, 2, and 1 or letters such as M (meets standard), P (partially meets standard), and D (does not meet standard). Instead of a final tally and letter grade at the top, you might provide a brief summary of the competencies and which scores they got for each competency.

Let Unwanted Systems Fade Away As You No Longer Need Them

When I ask teachers who have moved away from systems that use extrinsic motivation, "How did you stop using them?" a common answer I hear is some version of "Well, after awhile, I didn't need them anymore and they just kind of faded away." Once you build intrinsic motivation into work, teach students the skills they need to be successful, and stop focusing on the incentive systems, you might suddenly find that you're forgetting to pass out tickets in the hall or not having kids clip up or down depending on how they're handling the moment. This is a good sign that you can step back from the incentives.

Christine Cadieux Diaz teaches in the Chandler Unified District in Arizona. She explained to me that, at first, she wasn't quite ready to let go of her marble jar system. She and the students loved the marbles clinking in the jar, and the pizza parties and celebrations were really fun. Eventually, this changed. "As I became more proficient in reinforcing language, I noticed I was forgetting to drop in marbles and my students were less and less focused on pointing out they deserved one.... Now I was using brain breaks and we were having fun as a daily part of our routine, so the party wasn't something we needed for fun. It just naturally faded away." Notice that in order for this system to fade away, Christine used several replacement strategies. She infused fun into the day so that it wasn't something students had to earn. She also worked to recognize positive behavior through language instead of marbles. By saying to the class, "Wow! We just wrote for 25 straight minutes. We were focused and productive. Congratulations!" she could support the class's sense of competence while emphasizing what she really wants them to care about (sustained writing) instead of a pizza party.

Make Intentional Shifts Based on New Understandings

The other common answer I hear when I ask teachers how they shifted away from systems that emphasize extrinsic motivation involves a clear decision based on new learning. Devan Weber knew it was time to move away from using a clip chart where children clipped up or down according to their behavior after she read *Mindset* by Carol Dweck (2006). "Now that I understood more about mindset, I realized a clip chart strongly reinforces a fixed mindset. The 'good kids' were usually at the top, but everyone makes mistakes. If a child that saw themselves as a 'good kid' wasn't at the top of the chart at the end of the day, it was a catastrophic blow to their understanding of themselves, the result of which was crying meltdowns (often at home) and overzealously trying to outdo other kids to get to the top the following day. It was really bad." Her switch? Devan started using language to support students' positive actions. She said things like "How did it make you feel when you stacked the chair for Kelly?" and kept a checklist to make sure she was connecting with every student. Later in the year, she realized that the students had started to use these same kinds of comments with each other!

Michelle Galles teaches in a high-poverty school in Montgomery, Illinois, and she ditched her flip card system (where students flipped a card to a different color depending on their behavior, and different colors led to different consequences) after taking a three-day workshop about equity and then working with the Nurtured Heart Approach, which is based on the work of Howard Glasser. Instead of relying on consequences, Michelle talks with her students about "resetting," like in a video game. If a kid makes a mistake, they get to reset and try again. She also spends more time building relationships with students and recognizing lots of small positive behaviors in nonjudgmental ways. She says that, overall, students' behavior is much better, and she has a better connection with both her students and their families.

Jessica Fagan teaches in Portsmouth, New Hampshire, and she recounts a long list of incentive systems she tried. She started off with a marble jar. As a new teacher, she thought that's what she was supposed to do. There were times when she questioned if it was working. (When she told a colleague that after giving a marble for a good transition the next transition didn't go as well, she was encouraged to give more marbles.) She even began to resent the system because she felt so tied to it. Then clip charts hit the scene at her school, and she added that to her repertoire. She said it was devastating to see kids' names on the clip charts, and this made her question these systems even further. Finally, a colleague who refused to use either the marble jar or the clip chart system helped her rethink the whole system. It was the permission Jessica needed. Instead, she focused on really connecting with her students and building strong relationships with them. She realized later on that the marbles got in the way of authentic connections because the focus was on an inanimate object. Every now and then, the class throws a class party, just for the fun of it. It has been four years since she moved away from the marbles and clips, and she has no plans to go back.

David Davis is an instrumentals teacher in Minnetonka, Minnesota, with experience at the elementary, middle, and high school levels. He has recently been working at boosting intrinsic motivation in many ways. He used to choose all of the music for concert programs himself, but now he invites students to lend a hand, boosting their sense of autonomy and strengthening their sense of purpose. He also offers more choice on a daily basis through studio sessions, where students can work on pieces of their choice, and inviting students to bring in music from their own playlists to use for warm-up exercises. He used to assign workbook pages sequentially and offer achievement prizes and good grades for the students who completed the most. Now he uses the workbook as a resource and asks students which skills they are curious to learn about to supplement his planned lessons. Instead of using grades to judge students, he assesses *with* students through guided self-reflections. He used to consider himself a maestro who held sole power and control over the choice of instrument students could pick from, the selections of music they would learn, and whether they were performing up to his standards. Now, he views his role as a supportive mentor. His goal is to foster a love of music and support students in their musical journeys.

What has David seen as a result of these changes? He reports that students are practicing more voluntarily, so they are learning technical skills more quickly. Although he invested a good bit of time at the beginning of this shift, he says that his teaching is now more efficient because his students are more independent and can solve more problems on their own. His program has also seen significant growth, students are more likely to stay in his program once they start, and he has stronger support from parents and administrators (Davis, 2020).

Look for Small, Quick Wins

Jorge Ruiz is the new head of the International School of Sosúa in the Dominican Republic. He and I had an animated discussion about how schools can shift away from extrinsic motivation. One of the ideas he kept coming back to was to look for small wins—changes you can make quickly. He said that at his former school in Punta Cana, they were given the directive from the ministry of education saying that if they were going to give awards to some children, then everyone needed to get awards. "That was easy," Jorge said. "We got rid of the awards." He also got rid of the honor roll after faculty conversations revealed people's discomfort with honor being synonymous with kids doing their work. Once his staff had voiced their belief, the change was a logical next step. He helped students and parents understand the rationale for the change, but there was some tension. "How did kids react?" I asked. Jorge said that only the very "top" kids were bothered by it, so he sat down with them and helped them understand what colleges were really looking for—GPA, activities, interests, the courses students had taken, and so on. He told them, "Colleges look for who you are, not what awards you have received."

Jorge joined his current school in the midst of the COVID-19 pandemic, and he has already begun leading the school away from extrinsic motivators. He saw opportunities to help the school make some immediate shifts based on their new logistics. "I eliminated semester exams right away," he explained. Instead of using one exam as the primary summative assessment, he told teachers to use multiple formative assessments along the way—assignments, discussions, observations, and conversations—to inform semester grades. Instead of focusing on getting a grade on a specific exam, he wants students to focus on doing interesting work and teachers to focus on providing meaningful feedback throughout the semester.

This reminds me a bit of how I got rid of the chips for pizza system. I ripped that Band-Aid off. It was a quick and easy change that I could make right away.

So consider: Are there some quick wins right in front of you? Are there some immediate changes you could make?

Take the Long View

In addition to looking for short-term changes—ones you can make quickly and easily—Jorge also emphasizes the need to take the long view. He reflected on his own 10-year journey as an educator to really make the shift to his current understanding of motivation and importance of project-based learning. On his bulletin board in his office, he posts goals that run five years out from right now. He's mapping out a five-year plan to help his new school get to where he thinks they need to be.

Whether you're on your own personal journey or you're helping chart the journey for a school or district, make sure to recognize that meaningful change takes time.

Conclusion

Well, here we are. We want our students to be fired up and excited about learning, to learn deeply, and to be ready to tackle future challenges—in school and after they move on to other pursuits. Our goal is to help students develop the mindsets and skills they need to be successful, and the process is both simple and complex. It's simple because there are three ideas that can drive this work: Stop incentivizing learning and behavior. Activate students' learning through intrinsic motivators. Teach them the skills they need to stay self-motivated and to manage themselves effectively. It's complex because that's a whole lot harder than using incentives to motivate them in the moment, but in the end, it's also a whole lot better.

So how do you eat an elephant? One bite at a time. What will your first bite be?

Acknowledgments

It is with great thanks and appreciation that I would like to recognize many of the people who helped this book come to life.

First off, I'd like to acknowledge the work of Edward Deci and Richard Ryan and their work with self-determination theory, which has greatly informed the ideas in this book. The work of Dan Pink and Alfie Kohn has also been hugely informative and helpful. These researchers and authors have had a profound impact on my work as an educator, and for that, I am deeply grateful.

Thank you so much to my colleagues and friends—fellow educators who are also passionate about helping children love learning. Your willingness to share stories and advice, read parts (or even all!) of this manuscript while in process, offer feedback (both positives and pushes), and support my thinking has been invaluable. Through walks and runs around town, phone and Zoom calls, formal and informal conferences, you helped this book be better. To Susan Trask, Mike Fisher, Andy Dousis, Chip Wood, David Davis, Tom Newkirk, Chris Hall, Bena Kallick, Allison Zmuda, Daniel Hernandez, Leila Meehan, Kathleen Budge, Michael McSheehan, David Goldsmith, Jorge Ruiz, Jessica Fagan, Michelle Galles, Trisha Hall, Devan Weber, Pat Ganz, and Christine Cadieux Diaz, I extend a heartfelt "Thank you!"

Once again, thank you so much, Genny Ostertag and Liz Wegner. Your encouragement, guidance, and support have been so helpful. As you have several times before, you helped me take a jumble of ideas and a very rough draft and turn it into a cohesive whole. Thanks also to the whole ASCD team. Your professionalism and dedication to your mission help make the world a better place.

References

Anderson, M. (2010). *The well-balanced teacher: How to work smarter and stay sane inside the classroom and out.* Alexandria, VA: ASCD.

Anderson, M. (2016). *Learning to choose, choosing to learn: The key to student motivation and achievement.* Alexandria, VA: ASCD.

Anderson, M. (2019). *What we say and how we say it matter: Teacher talk that improves student learning and behavior.* Alexandria, VA: ASCD.

Anderson, M., & Dousis, A. (2006). *The research-ready classroom: Differentiating instruction across content areas.* Portsmouth, NH: Heinemann.

ASCD. (2014). Grading smarter, not harder: Tooth brushes and penalties [Video.] YouTube. Retrieved from https://www.youtube.com/watch?v=RsaXtN2-j54

Ayers, W. (1993). *To teach: The journey of a teacher.* New York: Teachers College Press.

Beilock, S. (2010). *Choke: What the secrets of the brain reveal about getting it right when you have to.* New York: Atria.

Benson, J. (2014). *Hanging in: Strategies for teaching the students who challenge us most.* Alexandria, VA: ASCD.

Berkson, E. (2005). The authentic teachers: The feelings that novice and veteran teachers experience in our schools. ERIC *Online Submission.* Retrieved from https://files.eric.ed.gov/fulltext/ED490710.pdf

Blauth, E., & Hadjian, S. (2016). *How selective colleges and universities evaluate proficiency-based high school transcripts: Insights for students and schools.* [White paper]. New England Board of Higher Education.

Brady, K., Forton, M. B., & Porter, D. (2011). *Rules in school: Teaching discipline in the responsive classroom* (2nd ed.). Turners Falls, MA: Northeast Foundation for Children.

Cain, S. (2013). *Quiet: The power of introverts in a world that won't stop talking.* New York: Broadway Paperbacks.

Calderon, V., & Yu, D. (2017, June 1). Student enthusiasm falls as graduation nears. *Gallup*. Retrieved from https://news.gallup.com/opinion/gallup/211631/student-enthusiasm-falls-high-school-graduation-nears.aspx

Cattani, D. H. (2002). *A classroom of her own: How new teachers develop instructional, professional, and cultural competence*. Thousand Oaks, CA: Corwin Press.

Center for Responsive Schools. (n.d.). *Responsive Classroom and PBIS: Can schools use them together?* [White paper]. Retrieved from https://www.responsiveclassroom .org/sites/default/files/pdf_files/RC_PBIS_white_paper.pdf

Charney, R. (2002). *Teaching children to care: Classroom management for ethical and academic growth, K–8*. Turners Falls, MA: Northeast Foundation for Children.

Collier, L. (2015, June). Grabbing students. *Monitor on Psychology, 46*(6). Retrieved from http://www.apa.org/monitor/2015/06/grabbing-students

Cosden, M., Gannon, C., & Haring, T. G. (1995). Teacher-control versus student-control over choice of task and reinforcement for students with severe behavior problems. *Journal of Behavioral Education, 5*(1), 11–27.

Crain, W. (2003). *Reclaiming childhood: Letting children be children in our achievement-oriented society*. New York: Holt.

Curwin, R. L., Mendler, A. N., & Mendler, B. D. (2018). *Discipline with dignity: How to build responsibility, relationships, and respect in your classroom* (4th ed.). Alexandria, VA: ASCD.

Davis, D. (2020). Shifting from extrinsic to intrinsic motivation [Blog post]. Retrieved from https://leadinggreatlearning.com/shifting-from-extrinsic-to-intrinsic-motivation/

de Barba, P. G., Kennedy, G. E., & Ainley, M. D. (2016). The role of students' motivation and participation in predicting performance in a MOOC. *Journal of Computer Assisted Learning, 32*(3), 218–231.

Deci, E., with Flaste, R. (1995). *Why we do what we do: Understanding self-motivation*. New York: Penguin.

Deci, E., Koestner, R., & Ryan, R. (1999). A meta-analytic review of experiments examining the effects of extrinsic rewards on intrinsic motivation. *Psychological Bulletin, 125*(6), 627–668.

Dueck, M. (2014). *Grading smarter, not harder: Assessment strategies that motivate kids and help them learn*. Alexandria, VA: ASCD.

Dunlap, G., DePerczel, M., Clarke, S., Wilson, D., Wright, S., White, R., & Gomez, A. (1994). Choice making to promote adaptive behavior for students with emotional and behavioral challenges. *Journal of Applied Behavior Analysis, 27*(3), 505–518.

Dweck, C. (2006). *Mindset: The new psychology of success*. New York: Ballentine Books.

Falk, A., & Kosfeld, M. (2004). Distrust—the hidden cost of control. CEPR Discussion Paper No. 4512. Retrieved from https://ssrn.com/abstract=590102

Fehr, E., & List, J. A. (2004). The hidden costs and returns of incentives—Trust and trustworthiness among CEOs. *Journal of the European Economic Association, 2*(5), 743–771.

Foster, C. (Producer), Ehrlich, P., & Reed, J. (Directors). (2020). *My octopus teacher* [Documentary film]. South Africa: Netflix.

Frey, B., & Jegen, R. (2001). Motivation crowding theory. *Journal of Economic Surveys, 15*(5), 589–611.

Fry, S. W. (2007). First-year teachers and induction support: Ups, downs, and in-betweens. *Qualitative Report, 12*(2), 216–237.

Glover, M., & Keene, E. O. (Eds.) (2015). *The teacher you want to be: Essays about children, learning, and teaching.* Portsmouth, NH: Heinemann.

Golinkoff, R. M., Hirsh-Pasek, K., & Singer, D. G. (2006). Why play = learning: A challenge for parents and educators. In D. G. Singer, R. M. Golinkoff, & K. Hirsh-Pasek (Eds.), *Play = learning: How play motivates and enhances children's cognitive and social-emotional growth* (pp. 3–12). New York: Oxford University Press.

Goodwin, B. (2018). *Out of curiosity: Restoring the power of hungry minds for better schools, workplaces, and lives.* Denver, CO: McREL International.

Greene, R. (2014). *The explosive child: A new approach for understanding and parenting easily frustrated, chronically inflexible children.* New York: HarperCollins.

Guirguis, R. (2018). Should we let them play? Three key benefits of play to improve early childhood programs. *International Journal of Education and Practice, 6*(1), 43–49.

Guskey, T. R. (2011). Five obstacles to grading reform. *Educational Leadership, 69*(3), 16.

Guskey, T. R., & Brookhart, S. M. (Eds.). (2019). *What we know about grading: What works, what doesn't, and what's next.* Alexandria, VA: ASCD.

Hare, B., & Woods, V. (2013.) *The genius of dogs: How dogs are smarter than you think.* New York: Penguin.

Hattie, J. (2009). *Visible learning: A synthesis of over 800 meta-analyses relating to achievement.* New York: Routledge.

Horner, R., & Goodman, S. (2009). Using rewards within school wide PBIS [Presentation]. Retrieved from https://www.pbis.org/resource/using-rewards-within-school-wide-pbis

Jensen, E. (1998). *Teaching with the brain in mind.* Alexandria, VA: ASCD.

Jolivette, K., Stichter, J. P., & McCormick, K. M. (2002). Making choices—Improving behavior—Engaging in learning. *TEACHING Exceptional Children, 34*(3), 24–29.

Kallick, B., & Zmuda, A. (2017). *Students at the center: Personalized learning with habits of mind.* Alexandria, VA: ASCD.

Kamenica, E. (2012). Behavioral economics and psychology of incentives. *Annual Review of Economics, 4*(1), 427–452.

Koenka, A. C., Linnenbrink-Garcia, L., Moshontz, H., Atkinson, K. M., Sanchez, C. E., & Cooper, H. (2019). A meta-analysis on the impact of grades and comments on academic motivation and achievement: A case for written feedback. *Educational Psychology.* Advance online publication. doi: 10.1080/01443410.2019.1659939

Kohlberg, L. (1981). *The philosophy of moral development: Moral stages and the ideas of justice.* New York: Harper & Row.

Kohn, A. (1993). *Punished by rewards: The trouble with gold stars, incentive plans, A's, praise, and other bribes.* New York: Houghton Mifflin.

Kohn, A. (2018, October 28). Rewards are still bad news (25 years later) [Blog post]. Retrieved from https://www.alfiekohn.org/article/rewards-25-years-later/

Kurtz, H. (2020, June 29). Survey: COVID-19 masks for teachers, but not kids; student engagement drops. *Education Week*. Retrieved from https://www.edweek.org/leadership/survey-covid-19-masks-for-teachers-but-not-kids-student-engagement-drops/2020/06

Land, G. (2011). The failure of success [Video]. TEDx Talk. Retrieved from https://www.youtube.com/watch?v=ZfKMq-rYtnc

Lepper, M. R., Greene, D., & Nisbett, R. E. (1973). Undermining children's intrinsic interest with extrinsic reward: A test of the "overjustification" hypothesis. *Journal of Personality and Social Psychology, 28*(1), 129–137.

Levitt, S. D., & Dubner, S. J. (2009). *Freakonomics: A rogue economist explores the hidden side of everything*. New York: William Morrow.

Lindblad, S., & Prieto, H. P. (1992). School experiences and teacher socialization: A longitudinal study of pupils who grew up to be teachers. *Teaching and Teacher Education, 8*(5/6), 465–470.

Maslow, A. H. (1943). A theory of human motivation. *Psychological Review, 50*(4), 370–396.

Meier, S. (2007). Do subsidies increase charitable giving in the long run? Matching donations in a field experiment. *Journal of the European Economic Association, 5*(6), 1203–1222.

Michael Jr. (2017). Know your why. Retrieved from https://www.youtube.com/watch?v=1ytFB8TrkTo

Middleton, M., & Perks, K. (2014). *Motivation to learn: Transforming classroom culture to support student achievement*. Thousand Oaks, CA: Corwin.

Moore, R. L., & Wang, C. (2021). Influence of learner motivational dispositions on MOOC completion. *Journal of Computing in Higher Education, 33*, 121–134.

Nelson, J. (2006). *Positive discipline: The classic guide to helping children develop self-discipline, responsibility, cooperation, and problem-solving skills*. New York: Ballantine Books.

New England Secondary School Consortium. (n.d.). 85 New England institutions of higher education state that proficiency-based diplomas do not disadvantage applicants [Webpage]. Retrieved from https://www.newenglandssc.org/resources/college-admissions/

Northeastern University. (2014). Business elite national poll, 3rd installment of the innovation imperative polling series. Retrieved from https:/www.luminafoundation.org/files/resources/pipeline-toplines.pdf

Piaget, J. (1946/1962). *Play, dreams, and imitation in childhood*. (C. Gattegno & F. M. Hodgson, Trans.). New York: W. W. Norton.

Pink, D. (2009). *Drive: The surprising truth about what motivates us*. New York: Riverhead.

Pofeldt, E. (2017). Are we ready for a workforce that is 50% freelance? *Forbes*. Retrieved from https://www.forbes.com/sites/elainepofeldt/2017/10/17/are-we-ready-for-a-workforce-that-is-50-freelance/#5553392c3f82

Redmond, P., & Solomon, J. (2007). Can incentives for healthy behavior improve health and hold down Medicaid costs? [Report]. Washington, DC: Center on Budget and

Policy Priorities. Retrieved from https://www.cbpp.org/sites/default/files/atoms/files/6-1-07health.pdf

Ritchhart, R. (2015). *Creating cultures of thinking: The 8 forces we must master to truly transform our schools.* San Francisco: Jossey-Bass.

Robinson, C. D., Gallus, J., Lee, M. G., & Rogers, T. (2019). The demotivating effect (and unintended message) of awards. *Organizational Behavior and Human Decision Processes, 163,* 51–64. doi: 10.1016/j.obhdp.2019.03.006

Rose, T. (2016). *The end of average: How to succeed in a world that values sameness.* New York: HarperCollins.

RSA. (2010). RSA ANIMATE: Changing education paradigms [Video]. YouTube. Retrieved from https://www.youtube.com/watch?v=zDZFcDGpL4U

Ryan, R. M., & Deci, E. L. (2000). Self-determination theory and the facilitation of intrinsic motivation, social development, and well-being. *American Psychologist, 55*(1), 68–78.

Sackstein, S. (2021). *Assessing with respect: Everyday practices that meet students' social and emotional needs.* Alexandria, VA: ASCD.

Sauer, S. J., Rodgers, M., & Becker, W. J. (2018). The effects of goals and pay structure on managerial reporting dishonesty. *Journal of Accounting, Ethics and Public Policy, 19*(3).

Schmidt, M., & Knowles, J. G. (1995). Four women's stories of "failure" as beginning teachers. *Teaching and Teacher Education, 11*(5), 429–444.

Shalaby, C. (2017). *Troublemakers: Lessons in freedom from young children at school.* New York: The New Press.

Sinek, S. (2009). *Start with why: How great leaders inspire everyone to take action.* New York: Penguin.

Skinner, B. F. (1976). *Self management of behavior* [Videotape]. Solana Beach, CA: The Media Guild. Retrieved from https://www.youtube.com/watch?v=kP8k_doYeGw

Slate School. (2020, May 13). Slate School Education Idea Lab: A deep dive into learner-centered education. Retrieved from https://www.youtube.com/watch?v=ZgMOKWHmEMY

Smith, D., Fisher, D., & Frey, N. (2015). *Better than carrots or sticks: Restorative practices for positive classroom management.* Alexandria, VA: ASCD.

Spencer, J., & Juliani, A. J. (2017). *Empower: What happens when students own their learning.* N.p.: IMPress.

Sujatha, R., & Kavitha, D. (2018). Learner retention in MOOC environment: Analyzing the role of motivation, self-efficacy, and perceived effectiveness. *International Journal of Education and Development Using ICT, 14*(2).

Teachers Throwing Out Grades. (n.d.). About [Facebook group page]. Retrieved from https://www.facebook.com/groups/teachersthrowingoutgrades/

Valiante, G. (2013, September 5). Alfie Kohn on Oprah [Video]. YouTube. Retrieved from https://www.youtube.com/watch?v=_6wwReKUYmw

Vatterott, C. (2015). *Rethinking grading: Meaningful assessment for standards-based learning.* Alexandria, VA: ASCD.

Venables, D. R. (2020). Five inconvenient truths about how we grade. *Educational Leadership, 78*(1).

Vygotsky, L. S. (1978). The role of play in development. In *Mind in society: The development of higher psychological processes* (pp. 92–104). Cambridge, MA: Harvard University Press.

Westerberg, T. R. (2016). *Charting a course to standards-based grading: What to stop, what to start, and why it matters.* Alexandria, VA: ASCD.

White, R. W. (1959). Motivation reconsidered: The concept of competence. *Psychological Review, 66*(5), 297.

White, R. W. (1960, January). Competence and the psychosexual stages of development. In *Nebraska symposium on motivation* (Vol. 8, pp. 97–141). Lincoln, NE: University of Nebraska Press.

Willower, D. J. (1969). The teacher subculture and rites of passage. *Urban Education, 4,* 103–114.

Wood, C. (2007). *Yardsticks: Children in the classroom ages 4–14.* Turners Falls, MA: Northeast Foundation for Children.

YouthTruth Student Survey. (2020). Students weigh in, part II: Learning & well-being during COVID-19. Retrieved from https://youthtruthsurvey.org/students-weigh-in-part2/

Yu, R. (2015). Choking under pressure: The neuropsychological mechanisms of incentive-induced performance decrements. *Frontiers in Behavioral Neuroscience, 9,* 19. doi: 10.3389/fnbeh.2015.00019

Index

The letter *f* following a page locator denotes a figure.

self-authored motivation, 16
self-determination theory (SDT), 15
self-interest, acting in one's, 21*f*, 22–24
self-management skills
    employment and, 3–4, 42–43, 75
    increasing motivation by teach-
        ing, 9
    intrinsic motivation and, 94–95
    teaching, restrictions on, 20
    when to teach, 80–81, 88
self-motivation
    grades emphasizing, 115–116
    level of academic engagement
        with, 22*f*
    true motivation vs., 4
self-motivation/-management, teacher
    characteristics for teaching
        flexible thinking, 76–78
        mindset of teacher as lead
            learner, 79–80
        patience, gratification delayed, 76
        self-reflection, 78–79
self-motivation/-management
    strategies, examples of
        be open to feedback, 84–85
        body position when working, 84
        breaks, 83
        build stamina over time, 87
        know when to stop working,
            87–88
        leave something unfinished, 83
        one bite at a time, 82
        procrastinate productively, 86
        recognize the blessing of a dead-
            line, 87
        screen out distractions, 85–86
        self-talk, 86
        set goals around time, not task
            completion, 82
        tackle an easy or a hard task first,
            82
        track your progress, 83
        turn off your inner censor, 84
        utilize productive times of day, 86

self-motivation/-management
    strategies, examples of—(*continued*)
        yoga poses, 83
self-motivation/-management strate-
    gies, how to teach
        common mistakes of, 88–89
        elicit ideas from students, 90–92
        fishbowl, 92–93
        modeling, 89–90
self-motivation skills
    employment and, 3–4, 42–43, 75
    when to teach, 80–81, 88
self-reflection quality in teaching
    self-management, 78–79
self-regulation, developing, 129–130
self-talk, using for self-management,
    86
shaming, 28–29
signaling
    distrust, 26–27
    values, 14–15
    work isn't fun, 67
simulations, 107–108
skits, 108
social and emotional skills, 132, 139*f*
stamina, building for self-management,
    87
standards movement, 40–41, 65, 76
strategy groups, 101–102
strengths-based feedback, 120, 124*f*
students
    cocreated learning, 98–100, 112*f*
    compliant, 4–5, 22*f*
    desire to do well, 126–127
    eliciting ideas from, 90–92
    goal setting in assessment,
        118–119, 124*f*
    norms and rules, cocreation of,
        128–129, 139*f*
    problem-solving, collaborative,
        135–138
    routines, cocreation of, 129–131,
        130*f*, 139*f*
    self-assessment, 119, 124*f*

About the Author

Mike Anderson has been an educator for more than 25 years. An elementary school teacher for 15 years, he has also coached swim teams, worked in preschools, and taught university graduate-level classes. In 2004, Anderson was awarded a national Milken Educator Award, and in 2005, he was a finalist for New Hampshire Teacher of the Year.

Now an education consultant, Anderson works with schools in rural, urban, and suburban settings across the United States and beyond. Anderson supports teachers and schools on a wide variety of topics: boosting student motivation, using effective teacher talk, embedding choice in everyday learning, blending social-emotional and academic teaching, and more. In 2020, he was awarded the Outstanding Educational Leader Award by NHASCD for his work as a consultant.

Anderson is the author of many books about great teaching and learning including *The Research-Ready Classroom* (Heinemann, 2006), *The Well-Balanced Teacher* (ASCD, 2010), *The First Six Weeks of School, 2nd Edition* (CRS, 2015), *Learning to Choose, Choosing to Learn* (ASCD, 2016), and the best-selling *What We Say and How We Say It Matter* (ASCD, 2019). His articles have been published in various resources including *Educational Leadership, Language Arts,* Teach.com, EdCircuit, and Edutopia.

Anderson lives in Durham, New Hampshire, with his amazing family: Heather, Ethan, and Carly. When he's not working, you might find him tending his perennial gardens, watching the Red Sox, or finding fun new places to run.

To learn more about Anderson and his work, visit his website: www .leadinggreatlearning.com. You can also follow him on Twitter @balancedteacher.

Related ASCD Resources

At the time of publication, the following resources were available (ASCD stock numbers in parentheses).

17,000 Classroom Visits Can't Be Wrong: Strategies That Engage Students, Promote Active Learning, and Boost Achievement by John V. Antonetti and James R. Garver (#115010)

Better Than Carrots or Sticks: Restorative Practices for Positive Classroom Management by Dominique Smith, Douglas Fisher, and Nancy Frey (#116005)

Cultivating Curiosity in K–12 Classrooms: How to Promote and Sustain Deep Learning by Wendy L. Ostroff (#116001)

From Behaving to Belonging: The Inclusive Art of Supporting Students Who Challenge Us by Julie Causton and Kate MacLeod (#121011)

Learning to Choose, Choosing to Learn: The Key to Student Motivation and Achievement by Mike Anderson (#116015)

Level Up Your Classroom: The Quest to Gamify Your Lessons and Engage Your Students by Jonathan Cassie (#116007)

The Power of Voice in Schools: Listening, Learning, and Leading Together by Russ Quaglia, Kristine Fox, Lisa Lande, and Deborah Young (#120021)

Teacher Talk That Matters (Quick Reference Guide) by Mike Anderson (#QRG120058)

Total Participation Techniques: Making Every Student an Active Learner, 2nd Ed. by Pérsida Himmele and William Himmele (#117033)

We Belong: 50 Strategies to Create Community and Revolutionize Classroom Management by Laurie Barron and Patti Kinney (#122002)

The Well-Balanced Teacher: How to Work Smarter and Stay Sane Inside the Classroom and Out by Mike Anderson (#111004)

What We Say and How We Say It Matter: Teacher Talk That Improves Student Learning and Behavior by Mike Anderson (#119024)

For up-to-date information about ASCD resources, go to www.ascd.org. You can search the complete archives of *Educational Leadership* at www.ascd.org/el.

ASCD myTeachSource®

Download resources from a professional learning platform with hundreds of research-based best practices and tools for your classroom at http://myteachsource.ascd.org/

For more information, send an email to member@ascd.org; call 1-800-933-2723 or 703-578-9600; send a fax to 703-575-5400; or write to Information Services, ASCD, 1703 N. Beauregard St., Alexandria, VA 22311-1714 USA.